# GOD'S BOOK
# OF POETRY

Other Thomas Nelson books by Herbert Lockyer:

*The Holy Spirit of God*
*The Keeping Power of God*
*The Power of Prayer*
*Portraits of the Savior*

# GOD'S BOOK OF POETRY

## Meditations from the Psalms

## Herbert Lockyer

Thomas Nelson Publishers
Nashville • Camden • New York

ISBN 0-8407-5862-6

# Contents

# 1

## The Psalms—
## God's Book of Poetry

Ever since I was a lad in school, I have loved poetry. Early in my life I developed a special love for God's poetry found in the Psalms. During the many years since then, I have studied and meditated on the Psalms. I have also enjoyed preaching on selections from the Psalter. I feel it is a deep privilege to be led by the Holy Spirit to expound to a congregation.

I recall the story of an aging seminary professor whose final words to his young ministerial students were something like this: "I envy you young men who have a whole lifetime to preach to God's people from the Psalms."

I, too, have been blessed with many years of preaching from the Psalms. Now I humbly pass along to you the fruit of my cultivation. I pray that this book will help you appreciate David, God's poet laureate, and learn spiritual lessons from him and the other authors of the Psalms. A blessing awaits you if you open your heart to the Holy Spirit as you open your Bible to the Psalms.

## Lives Touched by the Psalms

Poets and preachers have found exciting inspiration from the Psalms.

John Milton, when a lad of only fifteen, wrote this verse, based on Psalm 136:

> *Let us with a gladsome mind*
> *Praise the Lord, for He is kind:*
> *For His mercies aye endure,*
> *Ever faithful, ever sure.*

Testifying to the influence of the Psalms upon their lives and work, Bible scholars have described their appreciation of them in glowing terms. Martin Luther summed up the teaching of the Psalms in this characteristic fashion:

> In the Psalms we looked into the heart of all the saints, and we seem to gaze into fair pleasure gardens—into Heaven itself, indeed—where blooms in sweet, refreshing, gladdening flowers of holy and happy thoughts about God and all His benefits.

Bishop Horne, a devout student of Scripture and an author, designated the Psalms as:

> An epitome of the Bible, adapted to the purposes of devotion.... This little volume, like the Paradise of Eden, affords us in perfection, though in miniature, everything that groweth elsewhere, "every tree that is pleasant to the sight and good for food," and, above all, what was there lost, but is here restored, "the tree of life in the midst of the garden."

The study of the Psalter has engaged the minds of the most eminent, spiritually minded scholars of every age;

and for preachers desiring effective material for pulpit work, there is no lack of same, in the vast library of psalmodic literature they have made us heirs of.

For more than twenty years C. H. Spurgeon diligently studied hundreds of past works of the Psalms, and gave us the fruit of his labor in his incomparable *Treasury Of David*. As he finished this monumental task, the renowned London preacher confessed:

> A tinge of sadness is on my spirit as I quit *The Treasury Of David*, never to find on earth a richer storehouse, though the whole palace of Revelation is open to me. Blessed have been the days in meditating, mourning, hoping, believing, and exalting with David.

John Calvin, whose works Spurgeon revelled in, wrote in his preface to his own *Commentary on the Psalms*:

> What various and resplendent riches are contained in this treasury, it were difficult to find words to describe.... I have been wont to call this book not inappropriately, *an anatomy of all parts of the soul*; for there is not an emotion of which any one can be conscious that is not here represented as in a mirror.

As for St. Augustine, he stressed the necessity of having heart and lips in full accord with the truth of the Psalms, if we could study them aright.

> Attune thy heart to the Psalms. If the Psalm prays, pray thou; if it mourns, mourn thou; if it hopes, hope thou; if it fears, fear thou. Everything in the Psalter, is *the looking glass of the soul*.

James Gilmour, who went to Mongolia, bore a testimony to the influence of the Psalms in and over his life. Said this heroic ambassador of Christ:

> When I feel I cannot make headway in devotion I open at the Psalms and push in my canoe, and let myself be carried along in the stream of devotion which flows through the whole book. The current always sets towards God and in more places is strong and deep.

Ambrose of Milan revelled in the spirituality of the Psalms:

> Although all Scripture breatheth the grace of God, yet sweet beyond all others is the Book of Psalms. *History* instructs, the *Law* teaches, *Prophecy* announces, rebukes, chastens, *Morality* persuades; but in the Book of Psalms we have the fruit of these, and a kind of medicine for the salvation of men.

## Part of God's Holy Word

For the Hebrew, the Psalter is "The Book of Praises." Made up of 150 poems, the majority of which were set to music for worship by the ancient Hebrews, this collection became Israel's hymnal and prayer manual.

Our Lord and His early church were fond of the Psalms. Of the 289 quotations from the Old Testament that appear in the New Testament, not less than 116 are from the Book of Psalms. Some fifty Psalms are quoted. Early Christians were told to admonish "one another in psalms" (Col. 3:16).

With the dawn of Presbyterianism in Scotland, the metrical version of the Psalms, widely used during the Reformation under Martin Luther, became the hymns of the church. For years nothing save these ancient lyrics was sung in public worship.

10

As to the authorship of the Psalms, it is because David wrote the majority of them—some seventy-three—that the Book as a whole is referred to as "The Psalms of David." We have one psalm each from Moses (Ps. 90), Heman (Ps. 88), and Ethan (Ps. 89). The sons of Korah are credited with eleven, Asaph with twelve, and Hezekiah with ten. The remaining forty-two psalms are anonymous, but C. H. Spurgeon assigns all of these to David, "the sweet psalmist of Israel" (2 Sam. 23:1).

## Structure of the Psalms

The classification or arrangement of the 150 psalms into groups forms an interesting aspect of study. From ancient times the collection has been held to have five sections, or books. This very old Jewish statement expresses it: "Moses gave the Israelites the five books of the Law; and corresponding with these David gave them the five books of the Psalms." The whole collection, then, can be looked upon as forming a poetical Pentateuch:

Book One—Psalms 1–41. Corresponds with *Genesis*. Subject: *Man*—His state of blessedness, fall, and recovery.

Book Two—Psalms 42–72. Corresponds with *Exodus*. Subject: *Israel's Ruin* (42–49), *Redeemer* (50–60), *Redemption* (61–72).

Book Three—Psalms 73–89. Corresponds with *Leviticus*. Subject: *The Sanctuary*.

Book Four—Psalms 90–106. Corresponds with *Numbers*. Subject: *The Earth*.

Book Five—Psalms 107–150. Corresponds with *Deuteronomy*. Subject: *The Word of God*.

11

The Hebrew word *psalms* means "praises." The five books all end with praise:

Book One—Psalms 1–41. Ends with a doxology and a double *Amen*.

Book Two—Psalms 42–72. Ends with a doxology and a double *Amen*, with the addition, "The prayers of David the son of Jesse are ended."

Book Three—Psalms 73–89. Ends with a different kind of doxology and a double *Amen*.

Book Four—Psalms 90–106. Ends with a doxology, *Amen*, and *Hallelujah* ("Praise ye the Lord").

Book Five—Psalms 107–150. Ends with repeated *Hallelujahs* ("Praise ye the Lord").

## Studying the Psalms

There are at least four ways by which we can profitably study this precious collection of sacred hymns.

1. *Revelation*. First, the Psalms are seen preeminently as an unveiling of God as the Creator of the universe and as the covenant God of His redeemed people.

Throughout the Psalter, both the transcendent majesty of God and His imminent presence with His people are conspicuous. Such a revelation gives it height and depth unparalleled in any other book of praise. His holiness, omniscience, omnipresence, omnipotence, and righteousness are revealed. The storms may rage, but He sits on the flood, causing it to fulfill His purpose.

In a perilous time such as the world is presently experiencing in international affairs, with all the hatred, strife, bloodshed, and sin casting their shadows over world peace, how relevant is the revelation of God to the tangled skein of the world's history.

2. *Reflection*. The second way in which we can view the

Book of Psalms is to see how it reflects the inner hearts of those who wrote them, especially David. By the illumination of the Spirit he could find:

> Tongues in trees, books in running brooks,
> Sermons in stones, and good in everything.
> — Shakespeare, *As You Like It*

The Psalms reveal how those who wrote them could turn even the tragedies and the rugged experiences of life into forms of immortal beauty. As you reflect on the dark valleys and exalted mountaintops of their experiences, you may see your own pilgrimage more clearly.

3. *Relationship.* The third manner of approach to the Psalms is to trace their relationship to our Lord Jesus Christ, who could say, "These are the words . . . in the Psalms, concerning me" (Luke 24:44). While we have referred to the various writers of the Psalms, He was naturally their divine Author.

The Psalms, messianic in nature, must ever occupy a unique place in the praise-worship of the church because of their portrayal of Christ in His deity, humiliation, redeeming grace, and coming glory. He Himself used the Psalms in His own devotional hours and made them His textbook when instructing His followers in the mysteries of His person, work, and majesty. Once the disciples knew Him as the Messiah, they had no difficulty in recognizing Him in many of the Psalms.

4. *Religious Instruction.* The final way to meditate upon the Psalms is for our own personal enlightenment and edification. There is hardly any experience of religious life that the psalmists do not touch upon. In the language of their lyrics, our deep yearnings for God, our

contrition for sin, and our joy of sins forgiven find an echo.

Augustine relates with profound emotion what the Psalms meant to him when he became a Christian:

> How did I then converse with Thee when I read the Psalms of David—those songs full of faith, those accents which exclude all pride! How did I address Thee in these Psalms, how they did kindle my love to Thee, how they did animate me, if possible to read them to the whole world, as a protest against the pride of the human race? And yet they *are* sung in the world, for nothing is hid from their heart.

The Book of Psalms, then, is unique in that it provides you with adequate expression for your varied spiritual experience. If you learn the language of the Psalms, you will find it easier to express yourself in prayer. As you adopt the psalmist's attitude of consecrated praise, you will grow in your Christian experience. How blessed and enriched you will be when you make the confessions, prayers, aspirations, and praises your very own!

# 2

## The Psalm of Two Men

### Psalm 1*
### A Song of Introduction

The first psalm of the Psalter has a distinction all its own; it strikes the keynote for the entire collection of psalms.

Psalm 1 can be looked upon as the introduction or prologue or preface to the 150 psalms that form such a poetic section of the Bible. Psalm 1 is the text, so to speak; the rest of the Book of Psalms is the sermon or exposition on the text, and Psalm 150 is the conclusion. And like all suitable prefaces, Psalm 1 should be read first.

A further noticeable feature of this initial psalm is the way its six verses fall into two natural divisions of three verses each:

    1. The reward for saints (vv. 1–3)
    2. The retribution for sinners (vv. 4–6)

These parallel topics are impressive in that they epitomize not only the Book of Psalms, but the whole of Scripture. Since there are only two classes of people in the world—saints and sinners, or "the saints and the ain'ts"—this separation between the godly and the

---

*We suggest you read each psalm in your favorite version before reading Dr. Lockyer's comments.—EDITOR'S NOTE

ungodly runs through the Book of Psalms and the teaching of Christ, the prophets, and the apostles. The entire Bible reflects the two classes pointed out in this psalm. Isaiah wrote:

> Say ye to *the righteous,* that it shall be well with him: for they shall eat of the fruit of their doings. Woe unto *the wicked*! it shall be ill with him: for the reward of his hands shall be given him (Is. 3:10-11, italics mine).

The Gospels echo similar ideas:

> These shall go away into everlasting punishment: but the righteous into life eternal (Matt. 25:46; see John 3:36).

## *The Saint and His Reward (vv. 1–3)*

The opening word of this psalm is a favorite in the Bible, recurring with its cognates hundreds of times. The Hebrew word for *blessed* is a plural noun, and actually means "blessednesses." How bountiful God is in the reward of those who love and obey Him! What a chasm there is between the first and last words of the psalm—*"blessed"* and *"perish"*! They reflect the difference between the saved and the lost, and the gulf between heaven and hell. This first psalm, then, like the Beatitudes of the Master, commences with a benediction (or "good word"). May such a benediction be ours!

These opening three verses are unique in that they present both the negative and positive characteristics of the person richly blessed of the Lord. In verse 1 we have the things he will not do, while verse 2 describes the things he will do.

*Negative Characteristics.* As can be readily seen, verse 1 is made up of a series of triads, suggesting the three movements in failure. People seldom reach the depth of vice all at once. The life of a sinner is one of perilous progress downward. So we find three degrees of sin, with each depth leading to a deeper one.

1. *Ungodly.* Such a person may not be conspicuously sinful but is guilty of living his life without God. Usually, however, since he is godless he is restless, lacking in self-control and a victim of ungoverned passions. He is unconcerned about his own salvation and that of others.

2. *Sinners.* Here we have the general biblical term for wrongdoers. At the heart of this description of those who are far away from God is the idea of missing the mark, or failure to reach the divine standard of living. A sinner is one who comes short of the glory of God. One sinner is not like others. Each turns to "his own way" (Is. 53:6). Each sinner has his or her easily besetting sin. A drunkard may abhor a gambler, a gambler may abhor a prostitute, and so on.

3. *Scornful.* This is the last aspect of the progressive nature of sin. A sinner comes to the depth of sin when he not only *rejects* the only One who can save him, but actually *despises* Him. Only a fool mocks sin, eternity, and heaven and hell. This last state is worse than the first. Such bold and blatant impiety is the tragic end of a dreary journey away from God.

Connected with these three words are three movements to watch and shun—*walking, standing,* and *sitting.*

1. *"that walketh not in the counsel of the ungodly."* The true child of God is exhorted not to be unequally yoked with unbelievers. Why should any believer follow the counsel

17

of any unbeliever when he can have wiser counsel as he walks in the commandments of the Lord his God? If we allow our footsteps to be ordered by the Lord, we shall not be found following the cunning and wicked devices of the ungodly.

2. *"nor standeth in the way of sinners."* When a person starts to walk in the wrong direction and with the wrong company, it is not long before he or she yields to a complete fascination. Blood-washed sinners, professing to be renewed in heart, should only be found standing by grace in the congregation of the righteous. "Let the wicked forsake his *way*" (Is. 55:7), and all are blessed who stand not in such a way.

3. *"nor sitteth in the seat of the scornful."* If the ungodly man has his own self-evolved counsel and the sinner has his own particular self-chosen way, the scornful has his seat. The scorner may occupy a high seat, but it is near to the gate of hell. Boldest impiety is to be deplored. The Christian must be found outside such company. Sitting down suggests that the scorner has a seared conscience and is now a confirmed companion of unbelievers. At present the scorner may laugh God to scorn. The time is coming, however, when God shall laugh him to scorn and have him "in derision" (Ps. 2:4).

The New Testament presents us with a fitting illustration of a saint guilty of the three movements away from God. Peter, in his denial, walked away from Jesus. As he walked, he found himself listening to the false counsel of his Lord's foe. Reaching the high priest's house, Peter is pictured *standing* at the door, surveying the scene. Ultimately we read that Peter *sat* down with the scorners, warming himself at their fire.

Our only hope of safety is close and ever closer fellowship with Him who came to save sinners.

"Blessed is the man" is somewhat emphatic in the original, meaning *that man*—the man among myriads who lives for the accomplishment of the will of Him who created and redeemed him.

*Positive Characteristics.* We pass from what God's man will not do to what he will do—and must do, if he is to grow in grace. What an important *but* that is at the beginning of verse 2. It implies a strong contrast to verse 1, and seems to say, "On the contrary, here is a good man's character." His life is *delightful*, *fruitful*, and *successful*.

The first mark of a man who walks with the Lord, who stands for Him, and who is seated by Him in the heavenlies is that of a passion for His infallible Word.

1. *"His delight is in the law of the Lord."* The "delight" in this instance is no temporary, effervescent emotion but a deep joy of the heart over what the law is in itself—namely, holy, just, and good. Certainly the promises of Scripture give us much pleasure, because our delight is *in* the law.

Do we find the reading of the law of the Lord a constant, delightful exercise, or is our reading of the Bible a drudgery? Do we find the reading of much of the Word dry and uninteresting? Do we have to force ourselves to read because as Christians we know we should read it? Jeremiah wrote about some to whom the Word of the Lord was "a reproach" and who had "no delight in it" (Jer. 6:10). If we do not delight in His Word, we might never know what it is to delight in doing His will.

2. *"In his law doth he meditate."* If we take pleasure in the Word, we shall ponder over it. Rejoicing, we ruminate. Ruminant animals are those that "chew the cud," or constantly work the grass with their jaws and thor-

19

oughly masticate it. Do we ruminate on the Word? Do we roll the precious promises under our tongues as sweet morsels?

Are we not in danger of bolting our spiritual food? It is necessary to "take time to be holy"; it is also necessary to take time with our spiritual diets. To race through several chapters a day in order to complete a schedule for reading the Bible through in a year, and to gather little nourishment as we skip over the pasture, is not *meditation.*

This psalm in general, and this verse in particular, were favorites of Jerome. He translated it in this way:

> But his delight is in the law of the Lord; and in his law will he exercise himself day and night.

Meditation, then, means to "chew the cud," thus absorbing the sweetness and nutritive virtue of the Word into our hearts and lives and producing much fruit. The renowned preacher Thomas Watson expressed it this way:

> Meditation is the touchstone of a Christian; it shows what metal he is made of. It is a spiritual index; the index shows what is in a book, so meditation shows what is in the heart.

3. *"day and night."* Such profitable meditation is not to be an occasional exercise we engage in only when we feel like it. It should be a daily delight. As we read the Bible in the morning, it is helpful to choose a text and turn it over in our minds through the day. In this way, the Word becomes daily bread. Our days are always well spent when they are opened and closed with portions of Scripture. The Christian will profit from study, says

C. H. Spurgeon:

> In the *day* of his prosperity he sings *Psalms* out of the
> Word of God, and in the *night* of his affliction he
> comforts himself with *Promises* out of the same Book.

What must not be forgotten is that we have more to
feast upon than David had! All he possessed of "the law
of the Lord" were the first five books of the Bible,
although he dearly loved and continually devoured
what he had. How blessed and privileged we are with
the richer treasure of the sixty-six books forming the
complete revelation of God!

The results of a daily meditation on the Word and the
constant hiding of it in our hearts are of a threefold
nature:

1. *There is unfailing fertility.* "He shall be like a tree
planted by the rivers of water, that bringeth forth his
fruit in his season" (v. 3).

*Trees* are often used as a simile of the true believer, and
as the trees of the Lord they are always full of sap. Such
trees are *planted*; they are not wild trees growing without
attention. Did not our Lord warn us that, "Every plant,
which my heavenly Father hath not planted, shall be
rooted up" (Matt. 15:13)? But because we are chosen of
Him, planted in Him, and cultivated as His property, we
shall never experience the terrible uprooting Jesus
warned against.

As divinely planted trees, we have an abundant
source of sustenance, namely "rivers of water"—not a
single river, but *rivers*, which implies a never-failing
source. Our roots, like those of the Royal Vine at
Hampton Court in London, have a hidden source of
vitality. This is why such trees symbolize stability.

21

Their roots are grounded in the rivers of His grace, of His promises, and of His mercies. This is why we are able to bring forth fruit in season. When we love the Word and live it, we are bound to be fruitful in service. Fruit unto holiness is another outcome of close fellowship with the Lord over His Word.

2. *There is unfailing freshness.* "His leaf also shall not wither" (v. 3). Leaves beautify the tree. Ordinarily, when autumn comes leaves wither and die. But on God's living trees, the leaves are ever green and fresh. Kind words and deeds can never die, so says a children's hymn.

Prothero, in his *Psalms in Human Life*, quotes Rabbi David Kimahi, a noted Jewish commentator who lived well over five hundred years ago, who explained that rabbis yet older than himself interpreted the phrase "His leaf shall not wither" thus: "That even idle talk of a good man ought to be regarded—the most superfluous things he saith are always of value."

3. *There is unfailing favor.* "Whatsover he doeth shall prosper" (v. 3), or as *The Amplified Bible* translates it, "Everything he does shall prosper [and come to maturity]." Joshua also traced the connection between a passion for the Word and spiritual prosperity:

> This book of the law shall not depart out of thy mouth; but thou shalt meditate therein day and night, that thou mayest observe to do according to all that is written therein: for then thou shalt make thy way prosperous, and then thou shalt have good success (Josh. 1:8).

Blessed is the man who embraces such a promise! There is no reason to doubt that outward and secular success is included in such a promise. Soul prosperity, however, is what the believer longs for, and having this he is content with whatever the Lord may entrust him with in material things.

## The Sinner and His Retribution (vv. 4-6)

In this section of the psalm, look for contrasts between the righteous and the unrighteous. They are most conspicuous and sharply defined. The hopelessness of the state of "the ungodly"—a designation used four times in this psalm—is heightened by the portrayal of the prosperity of the godly in the first section.

The opening phrase of the last half of the psalm is most emphatic and is rendered in the Septuagint version: *Not so the ungodly, not so* (v. 4). The double negative is impressive, and implies that whatever those who are blessed of God have, sinners definitely do not possess. *The Amplified Bible* reads: "Not so the wicked [those disobedient and living without God are not so]."

First, there is the *character* of those without God. They "are like the chaff" (v. 4)—worthless, dead, without substance. The true believer, separate from sinners and loving the Lord and His Word, is serviceable to the Almighty. Those living without God are useless to Him. What a contrast there is between a massive, well-rooted, ever-fruitful tree and the rootless, fruitless chaff! Chaff, once separated from the wheat, has no value. Is this not a fitting description of the person who, while in his sinful condition, is of no use to God and of little worth in the world because of his self-centered life?

Second, there is the *condemnation* of the ungodly, "which the wind driveth away" (v. 4). Lacking the stability of a tree, chaff is carried through the air by the slightest breeze. The Chaldee translation for "wind" is *whirlwind*, suggesting the vehement tempest of death that sweeps away the soul of the ungodly, just as the flood waters suddenly destroyed the corrupt earth in the days of Noah. How solemn are the words of David in another of his great psalms where similar contrasts are used:

> [God] shall take thee away, and pluck thee out of thy dwelling place, and root thee out of the land of the living. . . . But I am like a green olive tree in the house of God (Ps. 52:5,8).

Behind the illustration of the wind bearing the chaff away is the Eastern mode of winnowing against the wind, when the light husks are blown away and the heavier wheat remains. Sinners are easily moved, disturbed, and the sport of any wind that blows. To use a modern phrase, the world "blows them away." If they linger and die in their sin, then there will come the winnowing by the fan of God's righteous judgment when, as the last phrase of the psalm expresses it, "the way of the ungodly shall perish" (v. 6). Such condemnation brings with it an eternal separation between the saved and the lost.

In contrast, we read, "The ungodly shall not stand in the judgment" (v. 5). *Stand in the judgment* is a legal term, meaning to maintain their cause in the trial. This sense is embraced in the translation of *The Amplified Bible*: "The wicked, those disobedient [and living without God], shall not stand [justified] in the judgment." Those who sit in the seat of scorners will not be able to stand before the righteous Judge at the Great White Throne. They will shrink before the Judge's unerring scrutiny. Then they will be without excuse and unable to stand in their own defense.

The "judgment" of those who are the Lord's at His *Bema*, "judgment seat" (Rom. 14:10), differs considerably from the position of those whose names are not in the Lamb's Book of Life. The service of saints is to be tried to discover its merit of reward; sinners will appear for the ratification of the condemnation already theirs, for "he that believeth not is condemned already" (John 3:18; see also v. 36).

Eternal doom consists in the blackness of darkness forever, with no possibility of ever being in the congregation of the righteous in heaven. Between the saved and the lost there is a great gulf *fixed*. Here on earth all congregations are mixed; tares grow with the wheat; saints and sinners meet together.

It is impossible to distinguish between the truly regenerated and those who are destitute of divine grace as you look out over a church gathering. Multitudes of church members are not members of His body. Their names are inscribed on church rolls but not in the Lamb's register above. But when "the general assembly and church of the firstborn" (Heb. 12:23) is complete in heaven, not one unconverted soul will be found in the courts above.

Without the new nature, heaven would be hell to a sinner. As Spurgeon expressed it:

> Sinners cannot live in Heaven. They would be out of their element. Sooner could a fish live upon a tree than the wicked in Paradise. Heaven would be an intolerable Hell to an impenitent man, even if he could be allowed to enter.

The concluding verse of this psalm is unique in that it not only summarizes the two sections, but it pictures the two companies and the two different destinies that await them. Our Lord taught that the straight gate and the narrow way lead to life eternal, but that the wide gate and the broad way lead to destruction. Further, He said that the travelers over the narrow way are "few" in comparison with the "many" journeying over the broad way (see Matt. 7:13,14).

*"The Lord knoweth the way of the righteous"* (v. 6). Who are the righteous the Lord attends to and provides for? Not those who clothe themselves in robes of righteousness of their own weaving. Such garments are as filthy rags in the sight of our most righteous Lord (see Is. 64:6). No, the righteous are those who have received His imputed and imparted righteousness, even Himself who is our righteousness.

The first half of Psalm 1 is descriptive of the character and reward of Jesus, the Righteous One.

*Knoweth* implies that His righteous ones have His special care. He is fully acquainted with everything concerning their lives and witness. "Mine eyes shall be upon the faithful of the land" (Ps. 101:6). The Hebrew of Psalm 1:6 is expressive: "The Lord is *knowing* the way of the righteous." His eyes are never off His sheep, even when darkness seems to hide His face. "He knoweth the way that I take" (Job 23:10). We do not know the way, but we certainly know the Guide, and we can trust Him who numbers the hairs of our head that all will be well. *Knoweth*, then, means to recognize with discernment and appreciation. "Thou hast known my soul in adversities" (Ps. 31:7).

*"But the way of the ungodly shall perish"* (v. 6). Here is one of those tragic *buts* of Scripture, so different from the *but* of the blessed in verse 2. Both the ungodly and his way perish. He leaves no fragrant influence behind. The

righteous carves his name upon the rock, but the wicked writes his remembrance in the sand. Job speaks of those who "go to nothing, and perish" (Job 6:18). Those who are Christ's "shall not perish" (John 3:16).

*Perish* does not imply annihilation or cessation of being, but to come to naught. "The expectation of the wicked shall perish" (Prov. 10:28)—come to nothing. The way and plans of the wicked end in disappointment and ruin. How solemn is this thought: "The LORD shall laugh at him: for he seeth that his day is coming" (Ps. 37:13). The end of the ungodly is "the ways of death" (Prov. 14:12).

Thinking of Jacob, Balaam said, "Let me die the death of the righteous, and let my last end be like his!" (Num. 23:10). For those there is the resurrection of life, but for the ungodly there is the certain "resurrection of damnation" or condemnation (see John 5:28, 29). Well might we echo the request with which Spurgeon concludes his exposition of this psalm:

> May the Lord cleanse our hearts and our ways, that we may escape the doom of the ungodly, and enjoy the blessedness of the righteous.

# 3

## The Psalm of
## the Messiah-Prince

### Psalm 2
### A Song of the Lord's Anointed

Can you guess why Psalm 2 was among Martin
Luther's favorite psalms? The psalm seemed to fit in
with the great reformer's defiance of his foes. Some of
his observations on this psalm throw into relief the
salient features in the character of the monk whose
very words were "half-battles." Consider this challeng-
ing paragraph from Luther:

> The Second Psalm is one of the best Psalms. I love that
> Psalm with all my heart. It strikes and flashes valiantly
> among kings, princes, counsellors and judges. If what
> this Psalm says be true, then are the allegations and aims
> of Papists stark lies and folly. If I were our Lord God, and
> had committed the government to my son, as He to His
> Son, and these vile people were as disobedient as they
> now be, I would knock the world in pieces.

As to the setting of the psalm, it has been suggested
that it was a hymn of glad victory used by the sons of
Korah to celebrate Israel's deliverance of the armies of
Jehoshaphat from hostile, bordering nations. Peter,

ascribing the psalm to David, applied it to godless rulers in New Testament times (see Acts 4:24–28), while Paul quoted it in his synagogue sermon on the theme of justification by faith (see Acts 13:33). Because of the nature of the psalm, it is applicable to godless persecutors of any time. Actually, the psalm is an extension of the old enmity between the two seeds God spoke of when He cursed the serpent in Eden (see Gen. 3:15).

We have already hinted that in ancient times Psalms 1 and 2 were treated as one, with Christ portrayed as the perfect Blessed Man in the former psalm and as the King's Son in the latter. Contrasts are indeed marked as we compare these initial psalms.

In Psalm 1 we have the contrast between the godly and the ungodly; in Psalm 2, the rage of the godless meets its doom in the reign of the Messiah. In Psalm 1 the wicked are blown away as chaff; in Psalm 2 they are broken in pieces as a vessel.

In Psalm 1 the righteous are as a stable, ever-fruitful tree; in Psalm 2 Christ is presented as the Head of the righteous and Rewarder of those who trust in Him. Psalm 2 ends where Psalm 1 begins, namely with "the blessed man."

Further, Psalm 2 is unique in these three particulars:

1. It is the first *prophetic* psalm. The establishment of David as king in spite of his enemies is a foregleam of the coming triumph and reign of David's greater Son— God's own Son—as King of Kings.

2. It is the first imprecatory or *judgment* psalm, breathing out terrible punishment upon the rebellious. The vials of wrath in the Book of Revelation constitute a full exposition of this psalm. If it lacks the Christian spirit of loving our enemies, it must be remembered that it was not written for a Christian age.

3. It is the first great *christological* or messianic psalm. It declares the pre-existence, deity, and reign of Christ. Professor Moulton points out that the motive of this psalm, and of other psalms of a similar spirit (87, 89, 110, 114, 132), is the mystic anointing of Jehovah's King to subdue and reign over the kingdoms of the whole earth. The King of Israel is to reign supreme as the Prince of the kings of earth, with Zion (Jerusalem) as the seat of His universal dominion.

Within the psalm, the sigh for dictatorship is met by the declaration of divine sovereignty. Here, the utter futility of opposing God is set forth in dramatic poetic form. The psalm falls into four stanzas of three verses each:

    1. Rage and Rejection (vv. 1–3)
    2. Derision and Decision (vv. 4–6)
    3. Jesus and Judgment (vv. 7–9)
    4. Instruction and Invitation (vv. 10–12)

## Rage and Rejection (vv. 1–3)

In the first three verses of the psalm, look for a vivid description of the innate hatred of human nature for God and His beloved Son. Such ancient satanically inspired antagonism is set forth in a fivefold way.

1. *It is malicious.* The writer, rightly amazed at the sight of puny creatures in defiance of the mighty Creator, commences the psalm somewhat abruptly with the angry interrogation, "Why do the heathen rage, and the people imagine a vain thing?" (v. 1).

On the Damascus road, Saul was breathing out cruelty against Christ and His followers. Such personal contagious hatred is illustrative of universal rejection of God and contempt for His Christ (see Acts 4:27,28).

31

*The Amplified Bible* translates the opening phrase of the psalm, "Why do the nations assemble with commotion [uproar and confusion of voices]?" How descriptive this is of international life today! The raging uproar and destruction associated with noisy demonstrations and mob violence surely tie in with what Jesus said about "the sea and the waves roaring" (Luke 21:25).

In the external agitation of a disturbed internal feeling, such as the psalmist's reference to the raging nations suggests, there is an allusion to the roaring of a turbulent sea. This metaphor is often used as a symbol of national commotion and upheaval. When Paul quoted this opening verse, the word he employed for "rage" denotes restiveness, as of high-mettled horses neighing as they rush into battle. Such is the spirit of those who rebel against God.

2. *It is deliberate.* The word *imagine* means to meditate and implies a mental decision. Thus, the psalmist asks this question: "Why do the people imagine, conspire, meditate upon, and devise an empty scheme?" Here we have not a mere thoughtless rejection of divine benefits but a considered, calculated opposition to all God is in Himself and to what He so freely offers mankind.

Human rage, however, is a bubble that quickly bursts. The evil "imagination of man's heart" (Gen. 8:21) is vain, empty, and comes to naught. Schemes to overthrow God and destroy Christianity ever end in failure. During the terrible Diocletian persecutions, a medal was struck by the God-hating emperor bearing the inscription, "The name of Christian being extinguished." What an empty boast that was! After the passage of centuries, there are more Christians today than ever before. The Christian faith will never have a burial place.

3. *It is resolute.* The hatred manifested by the people is

32

fostered by their leaders—"kings of the earth" and "the rulers" (v. 2). "Set themselves" indicates organized opposition, a banding together in a common cause. This is no temporary, effervescent rage, but a deep-seated, resolute hatred of God. For years Communist rulers have taken a stand together against the Christian faith. They have craftily and deliberately sought to destroy it.

4. *It is unified.* Meeting by appointment and counseling together, godless rulers seek the rejection of the Lord and His Anointed One, the Messiah. In the final battle of Armageddon, the same organized but doomed opposition will appear. "The kings of the earth, and their armies, gathered together to make war against him that sat on the horse, and against his army" (Rev. 19:19).

5. *It is rebellion.* The crowning display of human sin in its hatred of God is the effort to cast off every divine restraint. Humanity wants to be its own god. "Bands" and "cords" suggest restraints (v. 3). All over the world today there is a revolt against God and His laws. Sinners want to go their own way and will not suffer the Lord to reign over them. Where there is no vision, the people perish, or cast off all restraint. The divine yoke, so light and easy, is intolerable to godless and graceless hearts.

It is because of this revolt against God that we live in a world of growing international fear and increasing domestic crime. Behind all the rebelliousness of man is the sinister figure of Satan, the age-long, fierce antagonist who "didst weaken the nations" (Is. 14:12). As the time of his complete overthrow draws near, Satan will manifest great wrath against the Lord and His followers.

### Derision and Decision (vv. 4–6)

In the next section of the psalm (vv. 4–6), our eyes are turned from the council chamber of the wicked and the

33

raging, rebellious tumult of humanity to the secret place of the majesty of the Most High. Notice how vivid is the description of divine reaction to human contempt and rage! God, knowing that scorners cannot succeed in injuring Him or destroying His counsels, does not trouble to rise and scatter His foes. He simply "sits" and "laughs" at their expressive yet empty endeavors to get rid of Him (v. 4). How impressive is the composure and action of the Almighty!

*Think of His attitude!* First of all, He *sits* unperturbed, enthroned in quiet dignity far above all the malice and plots of earth, knowing He can do whatsoever He pleases (see Ps. 115:3).

He can afford to sit and wait, for His day is coming. The mills of God may appear to grind slowly, but they grind exceedingly sure. Seated, He *laughs!* So the God who included laughter in our physical makeup laughs over the irrational attempts of human beings to destroy Him. Man's vain rage excites divine derision. Heaven treats the hatred of earth as a joke. Is an elephant alarmed at the attack of a fly? The daring figure of God's derisive laugh indicates supreme contempt for man's empty boast. The day is coming when we will realize He mocks every threat of the wicked.

*Think of His action!* After His smile of derision He speaks in wrath. He has no need to rise and smite His foes; the breath of His lips is enough. Was not creation the result of His breath? He spoke, and it was done.

Over against the evil wrath of man there is the just wrath of God. How prophetic this psalm is of the Great Tribulation, when the wrath of God and the Lamb will be experienced by the godless of earth! Says dear old John Trapp, "He will vex them either by horror of conscience, or corporal plagues; one way or the other He will have His pennyworths of them, as He always has had of the persecutors of His people."

Among the many Roman emperors who distinguished themselves in the persecution and murder of the early Christians, several of them died tragic deaths. One of the most terrible foes of the ancient church was Julian the Apostate. In the days of his power, he pointed his dagger to heaven and defied the Son of God, whom he commonly called the "Galilean." But later on, when wounded in battle, Julian, knowing that his end had come, gathered up his clotted blood and threw it into the air, exclaiming, "Thou hast conquered, O thou Galilean!"

Similarly, Charles IX of France knew what it was to be vexed by God's judgment and sore displeasure. As the brutal monarch died, his agonies drove his blood through the very pores of his skin as he thought of his cruelties and treachery to the Huguenots.

What triumph there is in the phrase, "Yet have I set my King upon my holy hill of Zion" (v. 6). While the kings of earth set themselves in defiance of God, the heavenly Father speaks of His Son, the Messiah, as "my King" set or firmly placed in the seat of all authority.

Note the past tense the writer used—"*have I set*." Long before the outburst of man's hatred of God, Christ had been decreed as the King who "shall reign for ever and ever" and will yet be seen as the "King of saints" and "KING OF KINGS" (Rev. 11:15; 15:3; 19:16).

This is man's day—and a turbulent one at that! But Christ's day is coming when, taking to Himself His great power, He will reign unto the ends of the earth. Meantime, faith rests in the Omnipotent One, who is well able to outwit His crafty foes and make their follies the just sport of His infinite wisdom and power.

> *Thy foes in vain designs engage;*
> *Against His throne in vain they rage;*
> *Like rising waves, with angry roar,*
> *That dash and die upon the shore.*

## Jesus and Judgment (vv. 7–9)

In this section (vv. 7–9) another voice is heard. Through the first section of the psalm we heard the voices of kings and rulers as they plot in the council chambers against God and His Anointed. Then, in the second section we heard God's voice of derision and wrath from His throne above. Now, in this stanza of the psalm, it is the Anointed Son Himself who speaks and declares His rights of sovereignty, and warns the traitors of their doom. After God's derision of the wicked, you now may study the pronounced "decree of the Lord" (v. 7) and the challenge of His Son.

*There is His decreed and declared deity.* Christ is presented as "My Son" (v. 7)—a royalty and relationship recognized throughout Scripture. As the powerful Son of God, the Kingly One confronts the kings of earth with the decree that He will establish the very dominion that the angry nations strive to prevent. "I will declare the decree of the Lord: He said to Me, You are My Son; this day [I declare] I have begotten You" (v. 7, *Amplified Bible*).

Here we have one of the clearest and most explicit statements of our Lord Jesus Christ's glorious deity to be found in Scripture. *"You are My Son"* announced God the Father. Nothing could be more emphatic than that.

Much controversy, however, has raged around the phrase, "This day have I begotten Thee." The Son is begotten eternally before all time; there never was a time when He was not! As the filial relationship

36

between Father and Son belongs to the realm of mystery, it is more profitable to adore than argue, to believe than explain. Spurgeon fittingly observes at this point in his exposition of the psalm:

> If this refers to the Godhead of our Lord, let us not attempt to fathom it, for it is a great truth, a truth reverently to be received, but not irreverently to be scanned. It may be added, that if this relates to the Begotten One in His human nature, we must here also rejoice in the mystery, but not attempt to violate its sanctity by intrusive prying into the secrets of the Eternal God. The things which are revealed are enough, without venturing into vain speculations. In attempting to define the Trinity, or unveil the essence of Deity, many men have lost themselves: here great ships have floundered. What have we to do in such a sea with our frail skiffs?

*There is His demand for dominion.* As it was a custom among kings to give their favored courtiers whatever they asked (see Esth. 5:6; Matt. 14:7), so God says to His Son, "Ask of me" (v. 8). Jesus, in His teaching on *prayer,* assured His followers that if they asked they would receive. "Ye have not, because ye ask not" (James 4:2).

What did He request of the Father? Nothing less than His very enemies as His inheritance and the uttermost parts of the earth as His possession. It has been pointed out that the words "thee" and "for" in verse 8 are in italics, which means that they are additions of the translator for the purpose of further clarity. The implication is that by some previous arrangement on God's part, He had already assigned the possession of earth and its peoples to Him whom He had appointed heir of all things.

All the Father *purposed* for His Son, He promises to

fulfil on His behalf. Not until His millennial reign, however, will His pierced hand wield the scepter of universal dominion. Then His visible kingdom will stretch from shore to shore.

But for what purpose are the nations given to Christ as an inheritance? This eighth verse has been the basis of many a stirring missionary prayer appeal. The church has been urged to intercede that millions in heathen darkness may be made the Savior's inheritance. Without doubt, God has answered such petitions, yet the context of the verse makes it clear that the rebellious nations are asked for—not that they might be saved but slain, broken with a "rod of iron" and dashed "in pieces like a potter's vessel" (v. 9).

The iron rod expresses the severity of divine judgment on all who flout the authority and sway of the omnipotent King (v. 9). When He returns to inaugurate His reign, is He not pictured as having a "sharp sword" in His mouth? At the judgment of the nations, despite the manifestation of imperial strength, godless kings and rulers will be dashed "in pieces like a potter's vessel"—not bruised, but broken and never to be mended. All will then be subject to Christ's terrible power (2 Thess. 2:8; Rev. 2:16,17).

The phraseology of the psalmist indicates that the punishment of the wicked will be certain, irresistible, terrible, complete, and irretrievable (see Ps. 110). Would that the rebellious of earth might seek His face in penitence and faith as the age of grace continues and be thus delivered from coming wrath!

> *Ye sinners seek His grace,*
> *Whose wrath ye cannot bear;*
> *Fly to the shelter of His cross,*
> *And find salvation there.*

### *Instruction and Invitation (vv. 10–12)*

In the last section of this psalm (vv. 10–12) the scene again changes. From the severity of the Lord, we come to His goodness.

Before the rod of judgment falls upon the kings and rulers defiant of all divine authority, they are exhorted to honor the One they have hated. As the fear of the Lord is the beginning of wisdom, true wisdom befits kings and judges as they obey Christ and yield Him homage as their Sovereign. The psalmist means this: "Act wisely; be instructed and warned."

Without delay, rebellious rulers must desist and yield cheerfully to the Judge of all the earth. What a different world ours would be if only all its kings, rulers, and judges were followers of the Lamb!

Because of the greatness of God and of His Christ, they must serve with becoming reverence and humility. The kings are told to serve the Lord with reverent awe and worshipful fear, to rejoice and be in high spirits, with trembling, lest they displease Him. What a sacred compound is holy fear mixed with joy! Knowing that because of His mercy we are not consumed, we rejoice with trembling. This great, prophetic psalm ends with an invitation and a benediction. "Kiss the Son.... Blessed are all they that put their trust in Him" (v. 12).

Notice the use of the powerful word *kiss*. In Scripture, the kiss is suggestive of at least four ideas:

1. Love among equals (see Gen. 33:4; 1 Sam. 20:41; Rom. 16:16; 1 Cor. 16:20).

2. Subjection to inferiors (see 1 Sam. 10:1).

3. Religious adoration in worshipers (see 1 Kings 19:18).

4. Filial affection (see Ruth 1:14). When Judas betrayed his Master with a kiss, he abused such a token of

affectionate love and devotion. To "kiss the Son" means to recognize His authority and to yield to His sway, to love Him, and to obey Him.

A parent says to quarreling children, "Kiss and make up." If grown sinners fail to "kiss the Son" and be reconciled to Him, then they must perish. "The way of the ungodly shall perish" (Ps. 1:6). How unspeakable must the full wrath of God be when the kindling of it "but a little" results in the destruction of the sinner (v. 12)!

For all who are reconciled to God through Christ, there is the benediction of saving faith. "Blessed are all they that put their trust in him" (v. 12). At the outset of the psalm we have the disastrous results of trusting in rebellious rulers. The psalm ends on the note that it is better to trust in the Lord than "to put confidence in princes" (Ps. 118:9).

Without such saving trust, ruin is inevitable. The whole gamut of human emotions is expressed in this psalm: rage, laughter, joy, love, trust. We need have no fear of God as a consuming fire if our trust is in His Son's finished work on our behalf and we are no longer at enmity with Him. Are *you* certain of a share of the blessedness of those who trust in Him with all their hearts?

> *Trusting Him while life shall last,*
> *Trusting Him till earth be past,*
> *Till within the jasper wall,*
> *Trusting Jesus, that is all.*
> *—Edgar Page Stites*

# 4

## *The Psalm of Sighs and Songs*

### *Psalm 13*
### *A Dirge of Sorrow*

For centuries the number *thirteen* has been treated as a number of ill omen, a sign of bad luck or calamity. The Turks so disliked the number that it was almost expunged from their vocabulary. The Italians never used it in making up the numbers of their lotteries. Sitting down thirteen at dinner, in old Norse mythology, was deemed unlucky because at a banquet in the Valhalla, Loki once intruded, making thirteen guests, and Baldur was slain. In America, many hotels have no thirteenth floor. Likewise "13" is not used as a room number.

The first mention in the Bible of this supposedly unlucky number is in Genesis 14:4, where we read, "In the thirteenth year they [the kings] rebelled." There is another thirteen not altogether sinister. It is the number of Psalm 13, with its record of faith ascending from sighs to songs, despair to delight, gloom to gladness.

As with many of the psalms from David's gifted pen, this short one may have been connected with events in the history of the sweet psalmist of Israel. After he had been anointed king by the prophet Samuel and before he was crowned, he was sorely tried by Saul's jealousy and persecution. David knew he was God's choice as successor to Saul. He knew that one day he would be recognized as the king of Israel. Yet as an outlaw or fugitive, fleeing from Saul, he would often cry, "How long, O Lord!"

Taken as a whole, this psalm uses the language of many a tried child of God, expressing their feelings amid perplexing and recurring trials. In his exposition of this ancient psalm, C. H. Spurgeon says that if we change the *o* to *i* in "long," we have not *how long*, but *howling*. Too often, the repeated cry of a troubled, impatient heart becomes a howling (see Amos 8:3).

An impressive feature of the psalm before us is the quick ascent from the depths of lonely sorrow to the heights of heart-joy. There is the rapid change of emotions alternating from deepest despair to profoundest peace, with the turning point being that of prayer. Consider the following outline:

1. Perplexity (vv. 1, 2)
2. Prayer (vv. 3, 4)
3. Praise (vv. 5, 6)

### Perplexity (vv. 1, 2)

These first two verses constitute one long sigh made up of the fourfold repetition of the phrase, "how long?" Such a cry, indicating great anguish of heart and an intense desire for deliverance, is an oft-repeated one in Scripture. Study the following similar questions:

How long will ye turn my glory into shame? (Ps. 4:2).
But thou, O LORD, how long? (Ps. 6:3).

LORD, how long wilt thou look on? (Ps. 35:17).
How long, O Lord, holy and true, dost thou not judge
and avenge our blood on them that dwell on the earth?
(Rev. 6:10).

Let us look closely at the four "How longs" of this
psalm's emotions, which many a child of God still
travels through.

1. *"How long wilt thou forget me, O LORD? for ever?"* (v. 1).
Here is grief as it seems to be. The person feels deserted.
Although honest, it is a most ungracious question to
come from the heart of a redeemed child of God. This is
the first expression in the Bible of God's forgetfulness
of His own. Israel had the promise, "Can a woman
forget her sucking child, that she should not have
compassion on the son of her womb? yea, they may
forget, yet will I not forget thee" (Is. 49:15). But here is
the king of Israel moaning, "How long wilt thou forget
me, O LORD?"

God's memory cannot fail. The butler forgot Joseph
and did not remember him, but such a lapse of memory
is not possible with God. The only thing He does forget
is our confessed sin. "Their sins and iniquities will I
remember no more" (Heb. 10:17).

David added insult to injury by adding, "for ever?"
Not for one single moment does God forget any child of
His. Having created and redeemed us, He has graven
our names "upon the palms of my hands" (Is. 49:16)—a
metaphor expressing unceasing remembrance. Has He
not promised never to leave nor forsake us? Then, if He
is always with us and is *in* us, how can He possibly forget
us?

2. *"How long wilt thou hide thy face from me?"* (v. 1). Such a
sigh expresses grief as it actually is. "Why hidest thou
thyself in times of trouble?" (Ps. 10:1). But a hidden face

is no evidence of a forgetful heart.

When adverse experiences crowd in upon us, the darkness seems to hide God's blessed face. Desperately we pray, but the heavens are as brass and His ear seems closed to our entreaty. If His eye is ever upon us, why does He not rend the heavens and hasten to our deliverance? "Verily thou art a God that hidest thyself" (Is. 45:15).

At Calvary, the cry wrung from the heart of the Savior, "My God, My God, why hast thou forsaken me?" (Mark 15:34) suggests that the Father's face was turned from His beloved Son as He bore the terrible load of the world's sin.

Yet His own are never out of His sight, even in the thick darkness that seems to remove Him. If, as you seek His face in your trial and sorrow, it seems as if His face is turned away from your deep need, remember that His eye is on the sparrow, and that He watches over you.

> *What if Thy form we cannot see,*
> *We know and feel that Thou art near.*

3. *"How long shall I take counsel in my soul, having sorrow in my heart daily?"* (v. 2). Have you experienced this kind of grief, continual and questioning? Trials can cloud the mind and warp the understanding. I like this translation: "How long shall I lay up cares within my soul?"

The counsels or devices of our own hearts offer no relief in the dark and perplexing hours of life. We must look away from self for relief and seek counsel at the bosom of the Lord. It is not in man to direct his step. The Lord alone is able to order our steps aright.

Is there not a poignant touch about the phrase,

44

"Sorrow in my heart *daily*"? We read of the promised punishment of Noph [ancient Memphis], which would have "distresses daily" (Ezek. 30:16). For some burdened hearts there seems to be no relief. Day after day they suffer, with the load becoming heavier with the passage of time. Yet the promise can avail on their behalf, "As thy days, so shall thy strength be" (Deut. 33:25).

All the time David was on the run from Saul, who sought his life, sorrow over the king's murderous intent was in his heart *daily*. He knew that his enemy would daily try to "swallow me up" (Ps. 56:2; see 42:10). Yet it was this same man of sighs who wrote, "Blessed be the Lord, who daily loadeth us with benefits, even the God of our salvation" (Ps. 68:19). And the day came when in David's heart his sorrow was transformed into a song.

4. *"How long shall mine enemy be exalted over me?"* (v. 2). A bereaved person usually feels persecuted. Everything offers opposition. The psalmist's feelings of persecution were based on facts. David was Saul's constant enemy. Weary with running from him, David often sighed for an end of Saul's envious hostility.

John Calvin's first act at Geneva was to introduce the singing of the Psalms into the worship of the Reformed Church. He himself turned to the Psalms in times of mental strain, as well as in the throes of pain and death. Among his last words were those expressed in this psalm of David, "How long, O Lord?" Such a cry of weariness expressed Calvin's lament for the calamities of the Huguenots rather than his own impatience of spirit to be loosed from the trammeling influences of life.

This fourth sigh indicates that behind David's problems there was a person. His fears arose from a sinister figure seeking his death. Behind all of Job's trials and

45

tribulations was Satan. Paul came to identify his grievous thorn as a messenger of Satan. Behind Peter's suggestion of taking an easier way than the cross, Jesus detected the guile of the Devil.

Tried and tested saints must not fret over evildoers, all of whom are inspired by the master evildoer himself. Our chief enemy is already a defeated foe, for at Calvary Christ stripped Satan of his authority. His head was bruised by the woman's Seed, and now by faith that blood-bought victory over the enemy can be appropriated by any saints harassed by those hostile to their witness.

*Prayer (vv. 3, 4)*

Having considered the psalmist's fourfold complaint, we now turn to his fourfold expression of entreaty and confidence. Sighs become supplications, and the only way to ascend from sighs to songs is by the aid of the spirit of supplications. Prayer has the power to resolve our perplexities and give us joyous and contented hearts. Let us closely examine the four phrases of supplication making up the middle stanza of the psalm.

1. *"Consider and hear me, O LORD my God"* (v. 3). These words represent progress. From the question of God's hidden face, we go to "hear me." In place of a question, we now have a quest. "Consider . . . me." Here the word *consider* implies "look toward me" or "have regard for me." As God's blood-washed children we are His first consideration, and He is most considerate as we find ourselves perplexed over His mysterious providential dealings. "Hear me"—His ear is ever open to our cry.

We never call upon Him in vain. He hears and answers our prayers in His own way! "My God." Here

David, emerging from the darkness of despair, expresses the pronoun of personal possession—*my*—even as his greater Son did in the moment of His bitterest agony.

2. *"Lighten mine eyes, lest I sleep the sleep of death"* (v. 3). These words helped a Christian of an earlier time put thoughts into words. Gregory of Decapolis tells the story of a Saracen, converted by a vision of the Lamb of God. This convert, under the guidance of a Christian teacher, learned the Psalter by heart. With a burden for the salvation of his own countrymen, the Saracen preached Christ to them. But they rejected his witness and stoned him to death. In his final agony he prayed, "Lighten my eyes, that I sleep not in death."

In another psalm, we find David murmuring, "The light of mine eyes . . . is gone from me" (Ps. 38:10). Constant sighing of heart damages one's spiritual sight. It may be that David was physically weak when he wrote this psalm. Perhaps his eyesight was dim from hiding in caves and dens, and sickness threatened to cut short his career in God's service. Thus he prayed, ". . . lest this sleep into which I am now sinking be changed into the sleep of death." Saul desired David's death, and the psalmist feared that his trials might end in death.

"Lighten mine eyes!" Is this not a necessary prayer for all to pray? Every sinner blinded by the god of this world should utter it. It is also the prayer *every* seeker after truth, every tried believer, and every dying saint can pray. Simeon was ready and willing to die once his eyes had seen the Lord in the face of the Baby brought to the temple. All who are presently beset by the mysteries of life need grace to see God in the dark and eyes of spiritual understanding to comprehend His ways.

3. *"Lest mine enemy say, I have prevailed against him"* (v. 4).

The believer today, as well as David in the past, does not want Satan's forces to seem victorious. There were times when it seemed as if Job's friends were right, that the patriarch himself was wrong and worthy of his extreme suffering and loss. Ultimately, however, he prevailed over them and emerged justified by God. It would seem as if the religious foes of Christ, and of Stephen, and of ten thousand martyrs, triumphed in the murder of the saints they hated. The enemies of the cross often prevail over its heralds, as in the tragedy of the murdered missionaries in the Congo and in South America.

Actually, they do not prevail because they only can kill the body. Presently, Satan, our great enemy, might seem to prevail against us. But in Christ who triumphed over him at Calvary, we are invincible. By faith, Satan can be bruised under our feet, and ever is as we appropriate Christ's victory. God's honor is at stake in our preservation and in the overthrow of our enemies. He therefore will undertake for us.

**4.** *"Those that trouble me rejoice when I am moved"* (v. 4). The word "moved" implies being cast down from a firm position. "I shall not be moved" (Ps. 10:6). Constantly fleeing from Saul, there was nothing firm or settled about David's position. How Saul would have rejoiced to see David completely thrown down!

Wicked men sometimes try to compose comedies out of the tragedies of those they hurt. Nero played his "fiddle" or lyre as Rome perished. How the enemies of the three Hebrew youths rejoiced when they saw those fearless saints thrown into the fiery furnace. Others rejoiced when Daniel was cast into the lions' den. But their glee quickly turned to gloom and their own doom. God knows how to turn the contempt of the enemy upon his own head. David was eager to have God's vindication. He received it when Saul perished, even though David mourned for him.

Did not Christ teach us that God avenges "his own elect, which cry day and night unto him, though he bear long with them?" (Luke 18:7). Therefore, let us leave our foes as well as our fears to Him who knows what is best for us. He will deliver us in His own way and time. When the ungodly see saints suffering heavily, those saints may be tempted to believe that the Savior they suffer for is indifferent to their need. They may wonder if He is the real Deliverer He was proclaimed to be. But at the opportune moment, divine vindication will occur. Hostile foes will be defeated.

What we cannot be too careful about is giving those who trouble us an occasion to rejoice when we carelessly stumble and fall by the way.

### Praise (vv. 5, 6)

In these last two verses, we breathe in a different atmosphere. The winter of trial and doubt and fear is over. The time of the singing of birds has come. Mourning and moaning give way to music; sighing, to singing. Several psalms commence with sighs and end with songs (see Pss. 6, 22, 69, and 77). Occasionally, we find a psalm beginning with singing and ending in sighs (see Ps. 95).

*"But I have trusted in thy mercy"* (v. 5). Here is one of those blessed contrasts of the Bible! Job could say, "Though He slay me, yet will I trust in Him" (Job 13:15). The same avowal of confidence came from the lips of David. He knew that because of the mercies of God he would not be consumed by Saul. Mercy, along with goodness, had

followed him through all the days of trial. "Blessed are all they that put their trust in Him" (Ps. 2:12). A clear morning breaks for those who trust in the mercy of God as they endure the midnight of an apparently silent heaven.

*"My heart shall rejoice in thy salvation"* (v. 5). The vindictive rejoicing of the enemy gives way to the grateful rejoicing of the godly over a divine deliverance. The term *rejoice* means "to shout as in triumph." David's joyous triumph came when after all his sorrows and sighs, Israel gave him his coronation as their king. Salvation produces music in the soul. The bells of the heart peal out their melody over a full salvation from all past trials and transgressions.

*"I will sing unto the* Lord, *because he hath dealt bountifully with me"* (v. 6). What a glorious conclusion to a psalm that started with much gloom! It will be noted that three times over David uses the designation "Lord."

In verse 1 he sighs unto the Lord. In verse 3 he supplicates the Lord. In verse 6 he sings unto the Lord. And do you not think the Lord prefers our songs to our sighs? All fear of God's indifference or forgetfulness is driven out. The soul basks in the sunshine of His bountiful care and love. The garment of praise takes the place of the spirit of heaviness. Patience and faith are rewarded. Instead of "sackcloth," he is clothed with "gladness" (Ps. 30:11).

The Lord knows when and how best to deliver His own out of the snare of the fowler. We can be assured that He will not keep us in the crucible of trials a moment longer than is necessary. David's periods of anxiety while being hunted by Saul lasted for almost eight years. The paralyzed man at the pool of Bethesda suffered from his physical disability for thirty-eight years before relief came (see John 5:5). The woman whom Christ healed had had her infirmity for eighteen years (Luke 13:11). Lazarus was only relieved of his poverty and sores by death "into Abraham's bosom" (Luke 16:22).

Have you sighed long for emancipation from your troubles, adversities, or afflictions? Does relief tarry? Keep looking up, for you will yet praise Him who is the help and health of your countenance.

Let us review the lessons of this psalm.

*Sighs* will be yours until you breathe no more. Perplexity and despair amid trials may be your experience, yet remember that the night shadows are good for the flowers.

*Supplications* must be intensified. If your eyes fail, may they still look upward. The cultivation of ever-increasing dependence upon God can bring you a summer after the winter of discontent.

*Songs* of praise and gratitude will deal the deathblow to all doubts concerning God's care and provision. With the psalmist, you too will know what it is to ascend from "How long wilt thou forget me?" to "He hath dealt bountifully with me." When the clouds seem to veil His face, don't give up. "Although the fig tree shall not blossom," take down Habakkuk's instrument and play a tune on it (Hab. 3:17–19). You will hear the same tones of trial to triumph in Habakkuk that you learned from David:

> Although the fig tree shall not blossom, neither shall fruit be in the vines; the labor of the olive shall fail, and the fields shall yield no meat; the flock shall be cut off from the fold, and there shall be no herd in the stalls:
>
> yet I will rejoice in the LORD, I will joy in the God of my salvation.

The LORD God is my strength, and he will make my feet like hinds' feet, and he will make me to walk upon mine high places.

# 5

## The Psalm of Three Books

Psalm 19
*A Song of the Heavens Above and the Law Within*

Solomon declared that to the making of books "there is no end" (Eccl. 12:12). From ancient times, when the thoughts of men were inscribed on bricks, tablets, and parchment, right down to our own age with its computerized forms of printing, countless millions of opinions have been expressed. Today thousands of volumes, large and small, leave printing presses all over the world, many of them (I think) not worth the paper used in their production. In the realms of literature, with a distinction all its own, stands the incomparable Book of Books—*the Bible*—which Jerome spoke of as "the Divine Library."

Psalm 19, which we are now to consider, is one of the outstanding in the Psalter because of its subjects, profundity, comprehensiveness, and construction. In it, I find three related "books" easily discernible:

    1. The Book of Nature (vv. 1-6)
    2. The Book of Scripture (vv. 7-11)
    3. The Book of the Heart (vv. 12-14)

The title of the psalm informs us that David was its

53

author. It was used by the master of song in the sanctuary for the use of assembled worshipers. How their voices must have ascended to heaven as they echoed forth praise to God for His manifold works! To the saints of old, Jehovah was God of the skies, God of Scripture, and God of the soul.

## *The Book of Nature (vv. 1-6)*

Look at the theme of the first six verses of the psalm—*creation*. This subject makes these verses a great natural Bible, made up of three leaves—heaven, earth, and sea—of which heaven is "the first and the most glorious, and by its aid we are able to see the beauties of the other two," as Spurgeon expressed it.

He continued:

Any book without its first page would be sadly imperfect, and especially the great Natural Bible, since its first pages, the sun, moon and stars, supply light to the rest of the volume, and are thus the keys, without which the writing which follows would be dark, and undiscerned. Man walking erect was evidently made to scan the skies, and he who begins to read creation by studying the stars begins the book at the right place.

David, as a child of God, heard the voice of God in His created works. As a shepherd lad caring for his father's sheep, he constantly dwelt under the glorious fabric of the universe—the starry host brightening the sky by night, and the sun with its morning splendor ushering in another day. For all we know, David may have written this notable psalm as he gazed at the sunrise one morning. By contrast, he may have penned Psalm 19 during the blazing heat, one midday in the fields. Living near to the heart of God and the heart of nature, he knew he lived in God's world. He therefore wrote about natural religion, or the witness of creation to God's existence and power, long before philosophers appeared to write long discourses on the glory of God's world.

Creation, it has been said, is God's braille for a blind humanity to read. Studying the majestic language David uses of the witness of the universe, we note these aspects of God's revelation in creation:

1. *It is specific.* The psalmist does not argue about God's association with creation but states explicitly that it is His "handiwork" (v. 1, see also Ps. 8). The heavens, with their millions of luminaries, declare God's wisdom and power and glory.

> *Forever singing as they shine,*
> *The hand that made us is Divine.*

Paul magnified God as the One "clearly seen" in creation (Rom. 1:20). All His works praise Him as *El*—the Mighty One. By the "firmament" we understand the entire atmosphere enveloping the earth, which is also "the Lord's" (Ps. 24:1). The word *showeth* means to set before the eyes as a picture, and what a masterpiece of a picture nature presents. No artist is able to paint her sunrise or sunset adequately. Her marvelous shades of color are her own secrets.

To the child of God, then, there is no contradiction between what man calls "science" and religion. While the Bible does not set out to teach science, all its declarations as to creation are in full harmony with all that is truly scientific. To quote Spurgeon again:

We may rest assured that the true "Vestiges of Creation" will never contradict Genesis, nor will a correct "Cosmos" be found at variance with the narrative of Moses. He is wisest who reads both the *world-book* and *the Word-book* as two volumes of the same work, and feels concerning them, "My Father wrote them both."

2. *It is incessant.* We cannot witness all the day and night on behalf of our Creator, but His creation never ceases to magnify Him. "Day unto day" and "night unto night," for almost six thousand years now His works have praised Him (v. 2).

To "utter" implies to pour out as a fountain, and the heavens and the earth have had a stream of testimony flowing on without a break. Death ends the testimony of a believer here on earth, but the universe has never known a break since God fashioned it (Gen. 1:2). The day is mutely eloquent of divine power and goodness, and the night with the glory of the starry heavens reveals the perfect knowledge of Him who is able to save us from the darkness forever.

3. *It is audible.* Daylight sun and moonlight stars are God's universal, traveling preachers. Their voices are heard in all languages and dialects in all the earth. True, creation does not have an articulate voice, yet the adoring heart, whether in America or Africa, England or China, can interpret its silent speech. Its language is that of signs. "Their line" (v. 4) suggests the sound of a musical chord, and the significant actions and operations of the heavens and the firmament have a melody reason's ear cannot mistake.

4. *It is glorious.* Amidst all the glories of God's creation, the sun has the preeminence of a mighty monarch commanding all other planets. The tabernacle of old represented the *shekinah* glory, and God set the sun in the tabernacle of the universe where it ever remains brilliant and supreme. David used two common figures

of speech to describe the influences of the sun in and upon the universe as a whole.

First, the phrase, "As a bridegroom coming out of his chamber" (v. 5). As the sun bursts forth to scatter the darkness, it comes forth as a bridegroom in glorious apparel, with a face beaming with joy. And a bridegroom the sun is, for it is married anew to the needs of the world.

Secondly, "as a strong man to run a race" (v. 5). With matchless regularity and unwearying swiftness the sun continues its course. It never pants for breath nor finds the race too hard to finish. What a champion it is! No wonder God is likened to the sun.

> *Thou sun, of this great world both eye and soul,*
> *Acknowledge Him the greater; sound His praise.*

This herculean bridegroom never tires. As a circuit preacher, it carries its influence to the boundaries of the universe. Earth, sea, and sky experience its vital force and benefit from its light and energy. John Milton used the words, "as a giant to run his course" when he penned the lines of *Paradise Lost*.

> *First in his East the glorious lamp was seen.*
> *Regent of day, and all the horizon round*
> *Invested with bright rays, jocund to run*
> *His longitude through Heaven's high road.*

That there is a parallel between the heaven of nature and the heaven of grace is evident from the fact that Christ is portrayed both as a bridegroom (Matt. 9:15; John 3:29) and a strong man (see Mark 3:27; Luke 11:22). The church is His bride, and she rests in the assurance that the gates of hell cannot prevail against her. Her Lover is all-powerful to champion her cause.

## The Book of Scripture (vv. 7–11)

Throughout the Bible, God's creation and commandments are interwoven. This is why spiritual truths are largely symbolized by natural objects, such as church messengers being likened unto "stars" (see Rev. 1:20).

In this middle section of the psalm, we go from the skies to the Scriptures, from luminaries to the law. David knew a great deal about these two great "books" of God.

Revelation came to the psalmist's adoring heart from the world and the Word. How some scholars today waste their time and talents trying to find discrepancies and contradictions between nature and revelation.

Ancient tribal traditions and ethnic legends give us conflicting accounts of the creation of the universe. Modern evolution offers an unproven theory of the developing creation of man. But the Bible is the only authentic revelation in the world of God's creative acts. Conflict between religion and science often arises because scientists develop their own theories as to the origin of the universe and of man, discarding what the Scriptures declare.

Dwelling upon the antithesis between the revelation of God in the heavens above and the law on earth, Professor Moulton reminds us that the union of these two ideas has impressed the most diverse thinkers of diverse ages.

The German philosopher Immanuel Kant is credited with saying that the starry heavens above and the moral law within him were the perpetual wonders to his soul. Wordsworth in *Duty* expressed a similar thought in the lines:

*Thou dost preserve the stars from wrong:*
*And the most ancient heavens through thee are fresh and strong.*

Psalms 103 and 104 are companion psalms celebrating God as supreme in the world without and the world within (see also Pss. 26, 27). Both the world and the Word, then, reveal the glory of God and contain divine instruction and blessings for our hearts. God's wisdom is in His Word, as His works are in His world.

Magnificent though the testimony of the starry heavens is, that revelation is not sufficient. We must listen to the voice from the throne above the skies. In our highly scientific age, scientists are concentrating efforts on exploring the heavens, forgetting that the main obligation in life is to prepare for heaven. In the central stanza of Psalm 19 (vv. 7–11), in which Scripture is extolled, two general aspects are discernible:

1. The nature and work of Scripture (vv. 7–9)
and
2. The value and effect of Scripture (vv. 10, 11).

1. *The nature and work of Scripture.* The characteristic feature of the first portion is the way David cast truth in double lines, each holding a triad of expression as well as a variety of designations of Scripture. In each of the phrases we have *title, attribute,* and *effect.* These can be seen in this tabulation:

| Aspect | Attribute | Action |
|---|---|---|
| The law | Perfect | Converts [restores] the soul |
| The testimony | Sure | Makes wise the simple |
| The statutes [precepts] | Right | Rejoices the heart |
| The commandments | Pure | Enlightens the eyes |
| The fear | Clean | Endures forever |
| The judgments | True | Righteous altogether |

Does not this portion constitute one of the most remarkable evidences of the nature and ministry of Scripture? David had so little of our complete Bible— the first five or six books at the most. But what he had he dearly loved, delighted in, and meditated upon day and night. Let us examine the expressions he used.

*"The law of the LORD is perfect"* (v. 7). By *law* we understand the great body of revealed truth given for our instruction regarding character and conduct. As God is perfect in Himself, everything from Him bears the imprint of His perfection. We hear too little about the perfection of Scripture these days. There are religious and irreligious critics who delight in parading its apparent imperfections. But since it is divinely inspired, the Bible has no flaw. If it were not perfect, it would not be able to convert or restore the souls of men. Every born-again believer, then, is a fresh evidence of the veracity of Holy Writ.

*"The testimony of the LORD is sure"* (v. 7). Testimony, used here in connection with God, constitutes the divine declaration of what He has done, is doing, and will yet accomplish. The term also indicates what we should be and do. Sometimes our testimony does not have the ring of surety and certainty it should. But God's testimony is ever sure, reliable, trustworthy, stable— different from the shifting judgments of human reason.

As the reliable revelation of God's mind is read, believed in, and appropriated, it makes those who are simple enough to take God at His Word wise unto salvation. Trusting what He says, we are blessed with heavenly wisdom. Accepting the Scriptures as being true in declaration, right in direction, and eternal in duration, we come to possess a wisdom not of this world and receive an enlightened moral judgment.

*"The statutes of the LORD are right"* (v. 8). This further name or appellation, "statutes" or "precepts," implies that as the Lord He has every right to enunciate and enforce rules relating to our specific duty and requiring our obedience. There is no mistaking these divine requirements; they are clearly and unmistakably marked out for us so that a wayfarer, although a fool, cannot stumble over them. Such statutes are not stern or impossible of realization. "My yoke is easy," said the Master (Matt. 11:30), and when that yoke is accepted the heart rejoices. As He is obeyed, He becomes our exceeding joy (see Ps. 119:111; Jer. 15:16).

*"The commandment of the LORD is pure"* (v. 8). The rules or the regulations of life are not grievous. Jesus delighted in doing the will of His Father. While the divine decrees are authoritative, they are "pure"—spotless, clean, without fault, clear as crystal. When obeyed, they become light to the intellect and joy to the heart. Did not the Master say, "If ye know these things, happy are ye if you *do* them" (John 13:17, italics mine)? It is only as we *do* that we can *know*. There is no other way to be happy in the Lord except in trusting and obeying Him. As our "leader and commander" (Is. 55:4), He has every right to expect the implicit obedience of His followers.

*"The fear of the LORD is clean"* (v. 9). "Fear" in this case is not frightened, slavish fright, as if God were a tyrant. It is worship and reverence based upon God's revelation of love, grace, and righteousness in His Word. Such a fear must become the settled habit of the soul. This fear is *clean*, having no foul spot, and therefore endures forever. "The fear of the LORD is the beginning of knowledge" (Prov. 1:7), and with the intensification of our reverent trust and worship, heavenly wisdom increases, reaching its perfection in heaven where we

shall fear Him as we ought.

*"The judgments of the LORD are true"* (v. 9). There is nothing capricious about God's sentences and decisions. As the Judge of all the earth, He is ever right in His pronouncements against sin and in favor of holiness. His judgments are never wrong or false but ever in keeping with His own righteous and merciful nature.

Added to the sixfold delineation of the Scripture in the verses just considered, we have a most remarkable collection of designations in Psalm 119, where all of its 176 verses (except vv. 122, 132) mention Scripture in a variety of ways. What a Scripture-glorifying psalm this longest one in the Psalter is! It is similar to this section of Psalm 19.

2. *The value and effect of Scripture.* We now come to the worth and work of the Word in the lives of all who love and obey it. In verses 10 and 11 we note four aspects: possession, pleasure, protection, and profit.

*There is possession.* The entire Word must be "desired" and then kept (v. 10). First of all, there must be an appetite for it, then the application of it to every phase of life. The tragedy of our time is that all too few have any hunger for Scripture. Without study, they assume what they have heard about Scripture. They live with loose thinking about it, and such loose thinking results in loose living.

*There is pleasure.* "Gold" and "fine gold," "honey and the honeycomb" (v. 10) speak of the treasure and pleasure to be found in the daily search of the Scriptures. Material gold today demands a heavy price, and because of its preciousness is stored in large quantities by various countries. Some men and women crave to be rich and store up gold or money in different ways, but David says that the contents of the Bible are more to be desired than the most valuable gold on earth. Truly, all its precepts and promises have a preciousness far beyond the value of earthly treasures.

There is pleasure as well as profit in hiding God's Word in one's heart. You discover this truth in the metaphor of "honey," which is pleasurable to the palate and likewise nourishing, as both David and Jonathan knew (see Ps. 119:103; Prov. 24:13). Honey dripping from the comb is the finest and purest. One can eat too much natural honey (see Prov. 25:16, 27), but we can never consume too much of the honey of Scripture.

*There is protection.* Many of the truths of Scripture are signposts warning us of the danger of delaying to obey the Maker of the rules, the Author of the Book. Solemn warnings both for saved and unsaved alike are to be found within its covers. Sinners are warned to flee from the wrath to come (see Ezek. 3:19; 33:8; Matt. 3:7). Saints are warned against heresy and disobedience (see Acts 20:31; Col. 1:28; 1 Thess. 5:21, 22).

*There is profit.* Obedience to all God commands brings a "great reward" (v. 11). We do not obey in order to be rewarded. A child should love to obey his parents because he loves them, and not for any present he may receive for his obedience. Yet there is a rich recompense of reward, both here and hereafter, for all God's children. His obedient followers believe that His Word is in the Bible from beginning to end, and by the Spirit they endeavor to walk in the light the whole of the Word reveals. The original for "warned" also carries the idea of *illuminated* or *instructed*—a further aspect of the effect of Scripture.

## The Book of the Heart (vv. 12-14)

How practical David is as he concludes his marvelous lyric in which he extols God as the Creator of the universe and the Author of Scripture! He is likewise the God of the soul, as well as God of Scripture and God of the skies.

If only church members were as well-versed in this third book as they are in the first two, how different their lives and their churches would be. It is possible for a person to be outstanding in his knowledge of the Book of nature, whether his bent is in the direction of astronomy, botany, biology, or other aspects of the universe, and yet be totally ignorant of the Book of Scripture and of the book of his own heart.

Others may give themselves to an understanding of Scripture and know little of natural and scientific subjects, and even of their inner lives. One can be a theologian and yet not be a born-again believer, and consequently handle Scripture professionally and critically in a detached form without any application of truth. Does not God Himself speak of those who handled the law but knew Him not (see Jer. 2:8)?

The thrice-blessed are those who study the Word to show themselves approved of God, and who through the constant application of Scripture to every phase of life become workmen who have no need to be ashamed. With them, the Bible passes into behavior. The Word received, in a sense, becomes flesh and dwells among men. After contemplating the glory of the heavens, recall that David naturally passed into Scripture, which contains the divine record of the origin of the universe. Then in the last two verses of the psalm, he moved into a study of his inner and outer life. David desired to have Scripture as a guide and help in character and conduct. The psalmist desired the God who created our wonderful world and who inspired holy men of old to give to the world His Word. People need the Word to cleanse and control their ways, words, and works.

An ancient philosopher gave us the adage: "Know thyself." But do we know ourselves as we are in the white light of divine holiness? As David pondered over the book of his heart, he was humbled by what he read. There he found many a stained page. Note the terms he used to describe sin. After describing the perfection of God's created works and the veracity of His Word, we have the somewhat startling and abrupt question commencing the final and personal section of this psalm, asking who is aware of his sins.

"*Who can understand his errors?*" (v. 12). A Hebrew scholar says that the original gives the question in a very marked and significantly abrupt form. "Error who marks? From unconscious sins clear me." Turning his eyes inward, David realized how far short he came of the glory of God. Acts of omissions or sins of ignorance can only be known as *errors* by the light of Scripture. We are responsible for our ignorance as well as our light. People err greatly when they do not know the Scriptures nor the power of God. Are we cognizant of our own personal errors of conscience, understanding, will, and affection? There are some who fail to understand their errors in respect to their estimation of Christ and the Scriptures.

"*Cleanse thou me from secret faults*" (v. 12). A person can be not only a stranger to God and to those around him, but to himself. The word *secret* here does not only mean the faults we keep secret from others, but also those we ourselves have no knowledge of.

There is a world of unconscious, undetected sin within the best of us. With clearer light, the unconscious becomes conscious. Endeavoring to walk in the light, we find the blood of Jesus keeps on cleansing us from sin as its memory comes to the surface of consciousness. Most certainly we need to be delivered from all the hidden, private sins we are haunted by. They are actually never secret because the eye of God is upon them. We should cry for clearer light, that we may discover how vile and full of sin we are. As the sun David extols chases the darkness of night away, so the light of Scripture penetrating the dark recesses of our beings banishes lurking evil. God is able to pronounce us clean and keep us so.

*"Keep back thy servant also from presumptuous sins; let them not have dominion over me"* (v. 13). To *keep back* means to be "kept guiltless from." What is this presumptuousness we are to be restrained from, the fatal brink from which we are kept? It can appear in wilful, intentional, and deliberate sins. David prayed not just to be cleansed from these but to be kept back from committing them. Ancient Jewish scholars distinguished all sins as those committed *ignorantly* and *presumptuously.*

Look at the difference. David's sin against Uriah was one of presumption, but Paul's persecution of the saints was a sin of ignorance. Presumptuous sins are those engaged in with deliberation and choice against the voice of conscience and the voice of God's Spirit. Therefore, they constitute rebellion against the God who hates impurity. Sins show a despising of His explicit commands. How tragic it is when these sins against knowledge have dominion over a person! Nothing but God's restraining grace can keep a wayward and impulsive nature in subjection.

A Hebrew scholar comments that the word *presumptuous* comes from the Hebrew root meaning "to boil up or over," and always represents proud or arrogant people. In other words, "Keep thy servant from the companionship of arrogant men, so that they may not get dominion over me, and lead me away from thy law."

There are theologians and scientists who are arrogant and presumptuous in their denials of the fundamental truths of Scripture. May the Lord keep us back from them!

At the *British Association for the Advancement of Scientific Knowledge*, gathering in Cambridge back in September of 1965, scientists and economists from all over the world met to discuss the progress and problems of the age. Dr. Magnus Pike, a well-known British scientist, gave a paper that supposedly forever toppled God from His throne and revealed how man had taken His crown. Dogmas about the nature of man and the purpose of his life, he asserted, must be revised.

For instance, the noble declaration of the *Shorter Catechism*—"Man's chief end is to glorify God and to enjoy Him forever"—must now read, "Man's chief end is to glory in his achievements and enjoy their benefits forever." As a follower of Darwin, Dr. Pike stated in a television interview that man was descended from the ape, that Christ was no more divine than man is at his best, and that Christ's resurrection never happened.

The rejection of this fundamental doctrine by the presumptuous scientist, of course, makes Jesus out to be a deceiver and a liar. Before His death, Jesus often referred to His resurrection. And afterward He could say, "I am he that liveth, and was dead; and, behold, I am alive for evermore" (Rev. 1:18). But in spite of the advance of scientific "knowledge," the truth enshrined in Scripture abides unaltered.

*"I shall be innocent from the great transgression"* (v. 13). What a Hydra-headed monster sin is! Errors, secrecy, presumptuousness, pride, and now transgression are only

some of its evil heads. The margin expresses it, "much transgression." The particular sin of idolatry is intended. If we are delivered from the dominion of our sins of ignorance, secret sins, and presumption, then we shall be blameless and clear of any form of idolatry. On the basis of confessed guilt we are covered with the mantle of divine cleansing and forgiveness. Spurgeon goes so far as to say that David in his affirmation of innocence "shudders at the thought of the unpardonable sin." Secret sin is a stepping stone to presumptuous sin, and that is the vestibule of "the sin unto death" (see 1 John 5:16).

From the quickened and cleansed conscience of verses 12 and 13, we pass to the confident heart of the last verse of the psalm. *"Let the words of my mouth"* (v. 14) begins one of the sweetest and most expressive, practical prayers of the Bible. The psalm has journeyed from the heavens above to the heart within, both being spheres in which God dwells. He inhabits not only the high and holy place but also the hearts of those who are humble and contrite (see Is. 66:1,2). The skies above my soul ever remind me of His power. The Scriptures within my heart constantly speak to me of His pardoning love and grace and of the necessity of being obedient to His will.

Two aspects of the child of God are mentioned in this concluding prayer—his words and his meditation—and two aspects of God Himself—Strength and Redeemer. David prays that there may be no contradiction between his mouth and his mind. He knew that he could not be acceptable in God's sight unless his talk and thoughts were in harmony. That lips may say one thing and the heart another totally different is brought out by David in another psalm: "The words of his mouth were smoother than butter, but war was in his heart" (Ps. 55:21).

How we need to pray for a watch to be set upon our lips! In a vivid way, James describes for us the power of the tongue (see James 3). If we would be mature then we must not offend anyone needlessly by word of mouth. Pious words of the lips are a mockery if the heart does not know how to meditate upon Him from whose lips "gracious words" always flowed (see Luke 4:22).

David had prayed for cleansing in the most secret part of his heart; now he prays that the meditation of that cleansed and controlled heart might ever be acceptable to the One who looks upon the heart. If our meditation is ever of the Lord, it is bound to be sweet and conducive to right speech. Such a prayer for harmony of lips and heart indicates David's consciousness of weakness in both directions and of the need for divine control of his entire being. The supplication also expresses the psalmist's faith in God to remove any discord between his speech and his inner spirituality. This is why he concludes by calling upon God as his *Strength* and *Redeemer*.

"*O Lord, my strength*" (v. 14). The words mean "my Rock." He is our firm, impenetrable Rock in whom we are safe from the sins that beset us. The term "strength," however, is often used of God in Scripture, and we like to connect it with "the strong man" (v. 5), which links Him to His creative works. As our Creator, He enables. As our Redeemer, He saves. Having created us, He ever remembers that we are but dust. Yet He has made every provision for us.

But creation, although wonderful, only cost Him His *breath*. He spoke, and it was done. When it came to our redemption, God had to give more than His *breath*; He had to shed His *blood*.

> *Twas great to call a world from nought;*
> *Twas greater to redeem.*

69

By His blood as the Redeemer, we are made acceptable in His sight. By His power as the Creator, we can be kept acceptable before Him. And as the Redeemer who shed His ruby blood for our sins, He merits our full obedience to all His claims, and our praise throughout eternity.

# 6

## The Psalm of
## the Shepherd

### Psalm 23
### A Song of God's Protection

Among all the 150 psalms, none has been read, sung, quoted from, and written about more than the pearl of psalms—Psalm 23. All down the ages the language of this psalm has been dear to the hearts of God's people.

The Twenty-third Psalm is rich in poetic beauty and enduring in poetic truth. Saints of succeeding generations have seen in this brief psalm a mirror of the motions of their soul. Perhaps this was why Saint Augustine chose Psalm 23 as the "Hymn of the Martyrs," which countless numbers of them quoted as they perished for Christ's sake.

Joseph Addison, 1672-1719, renowned English essayist, had a deep affection for David's "Shepherd Psalm." He wrote in the *Spectator* in 1712:

David has very beautifully expressed a steady reliance on God Almighty in his 23rd Psalm, which is a kind of pastoral hymn, and filled with those allusions which are usually found in that kind of writing.

Lord Byron, the poet, spent his childhood years at

Aberdeen where, under the teaching of a Christian nurse, he gained a love and knowledge of the Bible. He learned many psalms by heart, Psalms 2 and 23 being particularly attractive to his poetic mind. What a different record would have been his if only his life had been constantly regulated by the teaching of the Psalter he deeply regarded.

## *The Carer and the Carefree (v. 1)*

A characteristic feature of Psalm 23 is its use of the personal pronouns "my," "I," and "me," indicating that all the divine Shepherd is and has is for each of us as individuals. Another psalmist, Asaph, wrote that the Lord was the "Shepherd of Israel" (Ps. 80:1) but such a general, national acceptance of the divine character did not satisfy the man after God's own heart. He thought of the Lord as being his own exclusive property. Thus David used the pronoun of personal possession, "The LORD is my [my very own] shepherd" (v. 1). This is why the psalm has a personal message for *you*. If you are numbered among His sheep, you can place your finger on this first verse and claim the Lord as *your* Shepherd.

The figure of the Lord as Shepherd, expressive of the Lord's relationship to His own, is common to Scripture. In beautiful imagery, Isaiah depicts the coming Messiah thus: "He shall feed his flock like a shepherd: he shall gather the lambs with his arm, and carry them in his bosom, and shall gently lead those that are with young" (Is. 40:11).

Christ presented Himself as "the good shepherd" willing to die for His own, and able to defend and preserve them (see John 10:14). As the risen, glorified Lord, He is our "great shepherd" (Heb. 13:20) and "the

Shepherd and Bishop of your souls" (1 Pet. 2:25). When He returns to the air, it will be as "the chief Shepherd" (1 Pet. 5:4) to reward His undershepherds. When He appears the second time on the earth, it will be to shepherd the nations with a rod of iron (see Rev. 12:5). Was it not fitting, therefore, that the first to receive the announcement of Christ's birth as the Savior-Shepherd were the lowly shepherds as they watched their flocks by night?

Approaching a meditation on this ancient psalm, a fact that must be borne in mind is its association with David's early life when, as a shepherd lad, he cared for his father's sheep. Doubtless he wrote the psalm toward the sunset years of life. Looking back over those early days, many of his experiences were illuminated by the Holy Spirit, of whom David said, He "spake by me, and his word was in my tongue" (2 Sam. 23:2). With telling effect, the psalmist borrowed metaphors from the scenes and experiences of the pastoral life he dearly loved. In his lovely lyric, David used these metaphors to fittingly illustrate God's providential care in providing all that is necessary for His children who know His voice and follow Him.

The opening verse of this famous psalm that many learned to recite at mother's knee is actually an epitome of the entire psalm. "The Lord is my shepherd; I shall not want." Note that the remaining five verses elaborate upon what we shall never want as we abide in His will.

Somehow, we agree with a dear old saint's version of this initial phrase when she said, "The Lord is my Shepherd; He's all I want." As our Shepherd, He knows what things we need before we ask Him and is well able to supply each and every need. No lack of any necessary thing will be ours. There may be things we want but do not need and other things we need but do not want. Multitudes of lost sheep desperately need the Shepherd's salvation, but they do not want it. The promise is, "My God shall supply all your need" (Phil. 4:19). We must be willing, however, to recognize our need and accept all that the Shepherd freely bestows.

## Rest and Refreshment (v. 2)

*Rest* is provided: "He maketh me to lie down in green pastures." When caring for Jesse's sheep, it was young David's responsibility to choose the best possible feeding ground. Careful selection had to be exercised in the provision of beneficial resting places where the sheep could eat and sleep. Is it not encouraging to know that Christ has anticipated our every need and made provision accordingly? Do you not love the description of the pastures? They are *green*, suggesting fresh, life-giving nourishment. There is nothing scorched, dry, or parched about our Shepherd's provision; it is all *green*, fresh, and tender.

In our modern age, with all its stress and restlessness tending to the exhaustion of nerves and vitality, rest is a vital necessity. "To work without rest is like overwinding a watch," says F. B. Meyer. "The mainspring snaps and the machinery stands still." This was why Jesus said to His somewhat tired disciples, "Come ye yourselves apart . . . and rest a while" (Mark 6:31). Once hungry sheep are sufficiently fed with the good pasturage provided, they are content to lie contentedly among the fragrant herbage. What appropriate words, then, appear in the Christian hymn:

> *Not a surge of worry,*
> *Not a shade of care,*
> *Not a blast of hurry,*
> *Touch the spirit there.*
> —*Frances Havergal*

## Grace and Guidance (v. 3)

*Grace* is offered: "He restoreth my soul." Throughout the psalm the present tense is employed: "maketh," "leadeth," "restoreth," "prepareth," "runneth," indicating that the bountiful provision of the divine Shepherd never fails.

In any age, any saint can appropriate all there is in Him. He is the same yesterday, today, and forever. Surely these words are among the most precious in the psalm for those who are deeply conscious of the Good Shepherd's restoring grace.

Bear in mind that we have a mirror of David's early experience as a shepherd in this lyric of his. We can imagine how often he would detect a sheep missing from the fold. Leaving the rest safe in an enclosure, he would go out after the straying sheep and search for it until he restored it to the fold. Such an incident was illuminated by Jesus in His incomparable parable of "the lost sheep" (Luke 15:3–7).

How constant is our need of spiritual restoration! With the psalmist we have to confess, "I have gone astray like a lost sheep: seek thy servant" (Ps. 119:176). Because we are not always susceptible and obedient to the heavenly voice and leading, we stray in thought and deed. Neglecting the Word of God and private devotion, spiritual decay overtakes us. We need restoration to our first love. Unconfessed sin, unspiritual company, and

75

disobedience to the known will of God result in the loss of the joy and power of our salvation. We need the restorative processes of grace.

If one has journeyed far from the Lord and wandered into deeper sin, there is the reassuring promise that He will "restore to you the years that the locust hath eaten" (Joel 2:25). The Shepherd waits to carry the lost sheep back on His shoulder into full fellowship with Himself and restore the old-time joy and satisfaction in Him and in His service.

*Guidance* is also offered: "He leadeth me in the paths of righteousness for his name's sake" (v. 3). The repetition of the phrase "He leadeth me" suggests a dual guidance. He leads us to the sufficiency of food and waters of rest and likewise along paths of righteousness.

Reflecting upon past experiences among the sheep, David recalled how when they strayed and went their own unguided way, they ended up in some tangled thicket. Eastern shepherds knew how important it was to choose the right paths—ways that would not cut the feet or strain the muscles of the sheep. As our divine Shepherd is the Righteous One, He cannot act contrary to His own being or character—which is what "his name's sake" means. His counsel is ever consistent with His character. "All the paths of the LORD are mercy and truth" (Ps. 25:10).

*He* leadeth *me*! What extremes there are between these two personalities! He leads me out of my poverty into His wealth; out of my sin and wretchedness into His holiness and righteousness.

This precious link *leadeth* also describes the versatility of the shepherd. Sometimes, the shepherd precedes his flock and his sheep follow. At other times, the shepherd walks behind the sheep and prods them on.

Is it not blessed to know that the Lord is in front of those who love and trust Him, and that safe and sure guidance is theirs if there is no intervening space between His footsteps and their own? We may not know the right way ahead, but we know the Shepherd. As we closely follow Him, all will be well. Christ said, "My sheep hear my voice, and I know them, and they follow me" (John 10:27). May we ever know what it is to follow the Lamb wherever He goes! The stony road He leads us over may appear to be the wrong one, but if we are intent on following Him it must be the right road. So let us ever pray:

> *Lead Thou me on,*
> *O'er moore and fen, o'er crag and torrent, till*
> *The night is gone.*
> —*John Henry Newman*

## Courage and Comfort (v. 4)

Perhaps no other Bible image has made a more lasting or indelible impression upon the minds of saints than this one of the dark valley. Think of the consolation this verse has brought to millions of saints and martyrs!

Bear in mind the background David had in his memory as he penned this line about a ravine. He had seen many. Overhung with high, precipitous cliffs and surrounded with a thick forest infested with wild beasts, such a dark gorge filled timid sheep with dread. But their shepherd was alert, strong, and well able to protect them against their enemies. Tenderly, David compares this ravine to the experiences of God's people, who must pass through many a dark valley before they come to *the* final valley of death.

*The shadow!* What harm is there in a shadow? Just as

the shadow of a dog cannot bite and the shadow of a giant cannot kill, so the shadow of death cannot destroy. Even of the death of the conscience-hardened, the psalmist says they could meet it without a shudder. "There are no bands [violent pangs] in their death: but their strength is firm" (Ps. 73:4).

Thousands of martyrs could walk with befitting pace through such a valley without fear and with a triumphant song on their lips.

No believer should be afraid to die. Death is not a foe but a friend; not an end, but the opening of the door to a richer, fuller life. As He walked through the dark valley of His earthly life, our Lord was able to exemplify this psalm. At life's bitter end He had no fear. "Father, into thy hands I commend my spirit" (Luke 23:46).

*Comfort* also is mine, for "thy rod and thy staff they comfort me" (v. 4).

The long staff of the shepherd was shaped like a crook at one end. If a sheep crept too near the edge of a precipice, the shepherd would catch one of the animal's hind legs in the crook and draw it back. At the other end of the staff was a thick band of iron used to beat off the dangerous beasts lurking near the pasture where the sheep rested.

David recalled his encounter with wild, ravenous beasts as he kept his father's sheep. Did he not tell King Saul of the way in which he killed both a lion and a bear that had robbed the flock? (see 1 Sam. 17:34). The comforting thought is that we have the Lord's watchful and directing providence. If our feet are apt to stray, His loving hand uses the crook of correction to keep us in the paths of obedience. When we are beset by foes who would destroy us, He uses the rod of His omnipotence to protect and preserve us.

## Banquet, Balm, Blessings (v. 5)

*A banquet* is provided: "Thou preparest a table before me in the presence of mine enemies." There were "enemies" in the presence of poisonous herbs and weeds growing in the pasture which, if eaten, would prove fatal to the sheep. Quickly seen by the trained eye of the shepherd, such injurious mixtures were removed. Then there were the hungry beasts waiting to ravage the flock, and robbers lurking in the shadows bent on plunder. The shepherd, therefore, was ever on guard—alert and watchful.

How privileged we are to sit at God's banquet table and feast upon His bountiful provision!

> *He daily spreads a glorious feast,*
> *And at His table dine*
> *The whole creation, man and beast,*
> *And He's a Friend of mine.*

A table speaks of loved ones gathered together in fellowship. As they eat, they enjoy each other's company. What is the Lord's Supper? Is it not a table spread in the presence of our enemies? As we sit, fellowshiping together at the memorial feast, outside in the world are the enemies of the cross, who see no beauty in the Shepherd that they should desire Him. Yet you find an inner ring of defense that even the satanic enemy himself cannot penetrate.

*Balm* must also be included in the Shepherd's provision. "Thou anointest my head with oil." This simile has been interpreted in many ways—as the Eastern custom of anointing guests with precious unguents as they enter a hospitable home, as the anointing of prophets, priests, and kings with "the oil of holy anointment" as they were set aside for their respective offices, as the anointing the saints receive as they function as kings and priests, and as the divine anointing with the Holy Spirit and with power.

But while all of these applications are permissible, the direct interpretation of the anointed head is associated with the shepherd's care of his sheep. David learned by experience that sheep were very susceptible to sicknesses and fevers, or liable to be bitten by a serpent or torn by a wild beast. For such needs, the psalmist had at his belt a horn of healing oil or mollifying ointment. If the skin was bruised and broken, tenderly the wound would be washed and then soothed with oil.

Bless God, there is balm enough in Gilead for all our fevers and wounds! Is a bruised heart yours? Have you been torn by the trials and afflictions of life? Well, the Shepherd-Physician is near to apply the oil of joy for mourning and to adorn you with the garment of praise for the spirit of heaviness.

*Blessing,* abundant and overflowing, is also provided: "My cup runneth over" (v. 5). Attached to the shepherd's girdle was his cup, fashioned from the horn of an animal. When he came to a quiet flowing stream or pool of fresh water, before his sheep drank he would plunge his cup in the water until it overflowed, and then slake his own thirst. For David, this simple act became alive with spiritual meaning as he realized the abundant goodness of the Lord.

Can we say that the overflowing cup is ours? Far too many of us are content with a mere trickle of blessing. We are strangers to the "rivers of living water" the Good Shepherd provides for the sheep who know His voice (see John 7:38). He does not measure out His blessing drop by drop. His is the overflowing bounty for all who are thirsty enough to appropriate it. Do you have all and *abound*? Jesus came that you might have not only life, but life *more abundantly* and that your joy might be *full* (see John 10:10; 15:11).

If the dry, barren world around is to be transformed into the garden of the Lord, He must have more overflowing cups. We need lives so deluged with the lifegiving water of the Holy Spirit that wherever they go, they will spill over a blessing. God deliver us from hoarding what we have and know of His salvation! Having freely received, we must freely give.

### Goodness and Glory (v. 6)

What a heart-moving story there is of the martyrdom of the brave Covenanter, Richard Cameron. His head and hands were "hagged off with a dirk," thrown into a sack, and taken to Edinburgh to be nailed to the City Port.

The blood-stained head and hands were first shown to Richard's father, then a prisoner at the Tolbooth. When asked if he knew to whom they belonged, the old man, kissing the brow of his beloved son's severed head, said, "I know them, I know them: they are my son's, my dear son's." Then the aged Cameron added, "It is the Lord: good is the will of the Lord, who cannot wrong me nor mine, but has made goodness and mercy to follow us all our days."

*Goodness* in the present is ours. *Goodness* and *mercy* have been called "the two guardian angels, heavenly escorts, and God's sent messengers" commissioned to attend to each believer during all the days of his or her pilgrimage. But in keeping with the imagery of this psalm, is it not more fitting to think of goodness and mercy as the two

81

faithful sheepdogs the shepherd loved and valued? When a shepherd went before his sheep, doubtless his well-trained dogs at the rear kept the sheep from straying.

There is never a day in the pilgrimage of the child of God when the heavenly escorts of goodness and mercy are absent. *All*, not some, of our days—days of storm as well as sunshine, days of trial as well as triumph, days of pain as well as pleasure—He is there. Is *this* day, as you read these lines, one of tears, loss, grief, adversity, or disappointment? Then look behind you, for God's two escorts are following you, and the Shepherd Himself is leading you. So lift up your heart.

*Glory* in the future will be ours: "I will dwell in the house of the LORD for ever." What a glorious horizon! As a shepherd lad, David lived the life of a nomad. When anointed king, David still had no dwelling place. Because of Saul's jealousy and suspicion, David was a fugitive for more than seven years, hunted from cave to cave by Saul, who sought his death. In the affirmation before us, the psalmist thinks of the Father's home in which he will *dwell* forever.

In another psalm, David tells us of his desire to "dwell in the house of the LORD all the days of my life" (Ps. 27:4). In his shepherd psalm, he yearns to dwell in the same glorious abode forever. He wants the temporal to become eternal.

Do we share his homesickness for heaven? Are our lives lived on the heavenly level? Since we may be nearer heaven than we realize, may we be found living as children of the dawn, with our faces toward the sunrise.

Several years ago, Dr. Charles C. Lindsay, when minister of the First Presbyterian Church in Coldwater,

Michigan, wrote the following lines, which he read at the burial service of a nine-year-old boy.

## Thou Art Our Shepherd

Thou art our Shepherd
For Thou hast so named Thyself.
Thou hast promised to seek for the sheep that is lost
Until Thou hast found it and made it safely secure.
We who come to Thee today have lost just one little lamb;
Only one—yet to us everything.
We cannot find him—our strength is insufficient—
And we seek Thy help.
Help us, O Christ, Thou Shepherd of the Sheep!

How shalt Thou know him?
Why Thou must know him—he knew Thee.
He knew Thee and called Thee by name;
Yes, he called Thee his "friend."
He knew no fear in an earthly sense—
The dark, the storms of summer, the snows of winter—
They held no fear for him.
Why?
Because his hand was in Thy hand:
His trust in Thy love.
'Tis him that we seek.
Help us, O Christ, Thou Shepherd of the Sheep!

You do know him?
And he isn't lost?
He is with you—and happy—and safe?
His eyes are shining—his voice is singing?
He's learning lessons—to know why the birds fly—
Why the flowers bloom, and what makes stars twinkle?
Yes, that's he—our lamb that was lost.
But lost no more.
We thank Thee, O Christ, Thou Shepherd of the Sheep!

We can bear the loneliness now—
We can face the future unafraid,
With hearts that are calm and serene.
We have discovered that he has left us his treasure:
The faith and trust which he had in Thee.
It's ours now—
Ours to have and to hold—
Ours to bring us comfort and strength—
Ours to lighten the load.
It's not for long that we shall be separated,
That he shall be away;
For he has shown us the way—
The way to Thy celestial fold.
Prepare for us,
And welcome us, O Christ, Thou Shepherd of the Sheep!

# 7

## The Psalm on Deliverance
## from Depression

### Psalm 43
### A Plea for Vindication

When Augustine was baptized by Bishop Ambrose of
Milan on Easter Sunday, April 24, 387, Psalm 43 was
sung at the ceremony and used throughout his subse-
quent career. Augustine made the Psalms his lifelong
study.

Because of their similarity, Psalms 42 and 43 often
have been linked together, the latter being treated as a
fragment of the former. But I hold to the position that
the two are separate psalms.

Although it stands unnamed among the unnamed
songs of Zion, just as there are many unnamed saints
amongst God's choicest servants, we have no difficulty
in identifying David as its author. Who but the gifted
harpist could write, "Upon the harp will I praise thee, O
God my God" (v. 4)? Had not the psalmist perfected the
art of soliloquy, or the habit of speaking in solitude to
his own heart about his fears and his faith?

Taken as a whole, the psalm presents this threefold
division:

    1. The oppression of foes—*Outward* (vv. 1, 2)

2. The expression of faith—*Godward* (vv. 3, 4)
3. The depression through fears—*Inward* (v. 5)

### The Oppression of Foes (vv. 1, 2)

David had a long and bitter experience of being sorely oppressed by his foes. Those who assailed him are descriptive of those every true believer faces. What are some of these persistent enemies?

*An ungodly nation* (v. 1). The psalmist asked God to defend his cause against a nation that had lost God. David knew that a people destitute of the fear of God would have no scruples in injuring him or in treating him unjustly. So he appealed to God's justice and righteousness, as many a true believer does who lives in officially godless nations like Russia, Cuba, and China.

Do we not live in an age of growing godlessness in national life? A land like ours may not be as blatantly atheistic as communist countries, yet we suffer from a practical atheism, living as if there were no God to obey or glorify. As a nation we may profess to be religious, but actually we are godless in life and thought, with a tilt towards accusations of the true Christian faith and its demands.

If the godless world around misjudges our motives, we can go right to the bar of God, our Advocate, and plead for His vindication. "O Lord, thou hast pleaded the causes of my soul" (Lam. 3:58). In the long run, His is the only verdict that counts. Popular opinion may be against us, but divine estimation is what we must strive for.

*Deceitful and unjust men* (v. 1). Deliverance is sought. Deceit and injustice are deadly companions, like twin vipers. Can it be that David had Doeg or Ahithopel in mind when he penned this line? The Devil, as the arch-deceiver, is all too active today branding every phase of life with deceit. Treacherous dealings, broken covenants, and betrayed friendships characterize modern life. Describing the last days, Paul said that evil people would be found "deceiving, and being deceived" (2 Tim. 3:13).

The three terms used in the first verse, "ungodly," "deceitful," and "unjust," describe facets of evil. (Compare the gradation in Ps. 1:1.) The *ungodly* are those who, living without God, live only for the gratification of their worldly desires. The *deceitful* are those who, Judas-like, don the garb of friendship yet rob us of our possessions and/or our reputation. The *unjust* can be identified as those who are corrupt. They sin against all rights and privileges. What a mirror the daily newspaper is of the injustice of our time!

There is a wider significance in the phrase, "the oppression of the enemy" (v. 2). Satan is the foul enemy of mankind. Behind the cruel acts of dictators and the violence of criminals, we can detect his influence. Is it not blessed to know that Jesus came to deliver those "oppressed of the devil" (Acts 10:38)? Truly, He is the Deliverer, able to preserve His own from the craft and cruelty of all foes.

Think realistically. There are times when the soul is tried. The godly person puts his or her doubts in the form of the two *whys:* "Why dost thou cast me off? Why go I mourning because of the oppression of the enemy?" (v. 2).

But we must always be careful not to mistake our feelings for actualities. When we feel forgotten or forsaken, we must cling to His promise that He will never leave us nor forsake us. Like the Master, we must learn obedience by the things we suffer. Amid all testings, He is our Strength. Taunted by our foes' question, "Where is thy God?" we can triumphantly say, "He is strengthening me 'with might by his Spirit in the inner man'" (see Eph. 3:16). We can't depend on natural strength in self-defense against the foe. He girds us with spiritual strength for the battle, and through Him we are more than conquerors.

## The Expression of Faith (vv. 3, 4)

If the outlook is oppressive, the uplook is encouraging and heartening. Thus, in verses 3 and 4, David turns his eyes from His enemies to God and records a twofold expression.

1. *The expression of desire.* Surrounded with the ungodliness, deception, injustice, and oppression of God-haters, the psalmist asks God to guide him out of their hands. He longs to breathe freer air.

*Light* and *truth* are twin angels or guiding stars ever near to lead the child of God out of doubt into confidence. Once, when Thomas Chalmers was preaching in Edinburgh, a heavy thundercloud darkened the building and alarmed the audience. But Chalmers gave out Psalm 43 to be sung, beginning at this third verse, "O send out thy light and truth." Almost immediately the cloud parted and the sun shone.

How deep is our need of the *light* the Spirit imparts, and of the *truth* as it is in Jesus! Light reveals our need, and truth shows how the need can be met. The Lord Himself is both the Light and the Truth. In Him we find the place we need.

*The place of coronation,* "thy holy hill" (v. 3). This means to us the one God has "set my King" upon (Ps. 2:6).

*The place of communion,* "thy tabernacles" (v. 3). In Israel of old, the tabernacle in the midst of the camp was the evidence of the manifest presence of God. Christ came and tabernacled among us and offers Himself as our hiding place as we live in the midst of foes. No evil can "come nigh thy dwelling" (Ps. 91:10).

*The place of consecration,* "the altar of God" (v. 4). In the tabernacle in the wilderness, the Israelite approached God by means of the altar from which ascended the fragrance of the whole burnt offering, upon which both God and man fed with inexpressible delight. Christ is our Altar—our only means of direct access to God. David was not a ritualist and did not have in mind a mere national altar when he went "unto the altar of God." His soul yearned for full fellowship with God Himself; so he added "unto God my exceeding joy" (v. 4).

Thus, the only cure for all oppression without and depression within is a life with the Altar in it. "Then will I go" (v. 4). What a significant phrase this is! "Going unto" implies submission and friendship. We go unto Him to pay homage to Him as our Lord and to hand over our entire lives for Him to use. We go unto Him to consult and converse with Him as our Friend, telling Him all our fears, doubts, sins, and hopes.

2. *The expression of delight.* Throughout this psalm we have several pronouns of personal possession—six *mes* and seven *mys.* Unbounded delight is resident in the phrases, "God my exceeding joy" (v. 4) and "upon the harp will I praise thee, O God my God" (v. 4). There can be no deep settled peace apart from Calvary. God is not only the Giver of joy but Joy itself—"God my exceeding joy" (v. 4).

## *The Depression Through Fears (v. 5)*

There were moments in the experience of Martin Luther when he felt something akin to despair. He, too, asked with David, "Why art thou cast down, O my soul?" The previous verse left us with the psalmist's going up to God. Now he is cast down in soul, and verse 5 contains two further "whys":

"Why art thou cast down, O my soul?"

"Why art thou disquieted within me?"

Continuing his soliloquy, the writer chides himself because of his feeling of despair. The "why" of distress because of the oppressing foe in verse 2 has led to the "why" of discouragement of soul. How often have you felt cast off, allowing the blatant forces of hostility without to disturb peace within your heart? Note the two antithetical ideas in this last verse of the psalm.

*Discouragement through fear.* If we are the Lord's and have such a God as the psalmist depicts, can we not get some insight about the origin of our moods and tempers? If the Holy Spirit is in control of our temperaments, then no matter what changes there may be around us He can produce and maintain inner calm and tranquility.

Possessing God, and being possessed by Him, there should be no room in our hearts for dejection. If, however, we find ourselves in an unshakable depression, we shouldn't hesitate to get help from a pastor, counselor, or a Christian psychiatrist.

*Recovery through hope.* "Hope in God . . . the health of my countenance" (v. 5). Eight times in this brief psalm, David mentioned the God he loved intensely. A person who is mildly despondent may suddenly realize, "I've been too self-centered. Instead of a microscope on my own wounds, I should focus a telescope on God's greatness."

Opposed by foes, we should never be discouraged—because God has promised to avenge His own elect. Thus, we may know Him not only as the *help* but the *health* of our countenance; this truth appears twice in the previous psalm (see Ps. 42:5, 11). The God who made the human face knows that it is the index of the soul; we carry on our countenances the evidence of a struggle within. But hope in God is a wonderful skin lotion, well able to chase the furrows from the brow and the sad despair from the eyes.

David began his psalm with a sigh, but he concluded it with a song. He ends the conversation with his own heart on a personal note, *"my* God." Can you say, "He is *my* very own God, my Joy of joys?"

*I have no cares, O Blessed Will,*
*For all my cares are Thine.*

# 8

## The Psalm of Lovers

### Psalm 45
### A Royal Marriage Hymn

In all the coronation offices in Britain from Egbert down, the symbolic services are based upon this psalm, and others of a similar kingly nature: the oil of gladness, the sword girded on the thigh, the crown of pure gold, the scepter of righteousness, and the throne of judgment.

Notice the long title that appears above this psalm in the traditional versions. The word *Shoshannim*, meaning "upon the lilies," is a poetical title given to the noblest of songs, describing as it does the One who came as "The Lily of the Valley" and as "The Lily among Thorns." Lilies, emblematic of purity and loveliness, fittingly portray the sinless Christ.

Mention of the "sons of Korah" in the title indicates the service of the choicest singers for such a choice psalm. Perfect praise for the King must come from the best-trained choristers. Sanctified affections, however, are more important than musical voices.

*Maschal*, another part of the title, implies "instruction" and reminds us that this is no romancing ballad, but an instructive ode that only the spiritually minded can understand.

That it is a love song is evident from the last title given, *A Song of Loves*. The psalm as a whole is not a sensuous, sentimental love song, but a canticle of divine love, extolling Him whose love surpasses all others. I classify this as a messianic psalm.

As to the background of this royal psalm, while it may have had its origin in a marriage hymn of some Jewish monarch, he was but a hazy shadow of the glorious King who was born in Bethlehem's manger. Spurgeon says that those who only see Solomon and Pharaoh's daughter in the psalm are shortsighted.

Dr. Alexander MacLaren writes:

> We must admit one of two things. Either we have here a piece of poetic exaggeration far beyond the limits of poetic license, or "a greater king than Solomon is here." . . . The Psalmist sees the ideal Person Who, as he knew, was one day to be real, shining through the shadowy form of the earthly king. . . . In plainer words, the Psalm celebrates Christ.

The New Testament definitely relates the psalm to Christ. Quoting verses 6 and 7, the writer to the Hebrews has it,

> Unto the Son he saith,
> Thy throne, O God, is for ever and ever:
> a scepter of righteousness is the scepter of thy kingdom.
> Thou hast loved righteousness, and hated iniquity;
> therefore God, even thy God, hath anointed thee
> with the oil of gladness above thy fellows (Heb. 1:8, 9).

Thus, without any doubt whatever in my mind, I find the psalm is eloquent with the truth of the mystical union between Christ and His church. It gives me a picture of the King in His beauty and the queen in her glory.

For clarity's sake, this "lily" psalm can be outlined in the following sixfold way:

Description of the King (vv. 1, 2)
Dominion of the King (vv. 3–5)
Deity of the King (vv. 6, 7)
Dress of the King (v. 8)
Daughters of the King (vv. 9–15)
Decree of the King (vv. 16, 17)

### Description of the King (vv. 1, 2)

The entire psalm has the King as its subject, even though the latter half of the psalm is taken up with His family. Everything is the King's. Note also the pronoun *thy* as applied to the King and His possessions. It tells of His rightful ownership.

In the first portion we have a bubbling heart and an eloquent tongue. The word for *inditing* is "to bubble or boil." It expresses a warmth of love issuing in an overflow of utterance. There was nothing cold or frigid about the psalmist's feeling. With a full, warm heart, he was ready to sing of the King. With such a good topic, his manner was correct. He was ready as a writer to pen his tribute of the King with exactness and skillfulness of expression.

The psalmist's overflowing heart finds it easy to extol the superhuman excellencies of the King. He is lost in adoration as he thinks of the One who is fairer in person and character than any other. The literal Hebrew is "Beautiful, beautiful Thou art." The best of men are only men at best. Flaws mar the character of the most commendable, but the perfect Christ holds all graces in harmonious proportion.

*All human beauties, all divine,*
*In our Redeemer meet and shine.*

Godly Samuel Rutherford was surely possessed of the bubbling heart when he wrote:

> O fair sun, and fair moon, and fair stars, and fair flowers, and fair roses, and fair lilies, but O, ten thousand times fairer Lord Jesus! Alas! I have wronged Him in making the comparison in this way. O black sun and moon! but O Fair Lord Jesus!

Count von Zinzendorf experienced a similar ecstasy when he exclaimed, "I have a passion and it is He—He only." While physical perfection is before us, there is also a deeper reference to character, combining all sovereign grace and stainless purity. And yet although He was "fairer than the children of men" (v. 2), Isaiah said, "His visage was so marred more than any man. . . . there is no beauty that we should desire him" (Is. 52:14; 53:2). Yet brutal treatment could not hide His loveliness. Christ was never so majestic as when He was bound and blood-spattered, and Pilate cried, "Behold the man!" (John 19:5).

But the King portrayed in the opening verses of this psalm has eloquence as well as elegance. Not only does majestic sweetness sit enthroned on His brow, but "grace is poured into Thy lips" (v. 2). The Gospels are proof of His kingly graciousness in conversation. Never man spoke like this Man! One word of His was sufficient to turn winter into summer for dreary souls.

The word "poured" implies that He had fitting speech in abundance. Christ was a perfect man; He never uttered an offensive word. Citizens of Nazareth "wondered at the gracious words which proceeded out of His mouth" (Luke 4:22). Ever regal and authoritative in His utterance, He never forgot the need to be tender and kind. He exemplified the qualities of the ideal monarch, namely, personal beauty and courtesy of manner.

And the eternal benediction of the Father is His reward for all His loveliness and graciousness. "Therefore God hath blessed thee for ever" (v. 2).

### Dominion of the King (vv. 3-5)

Passing from the person of the King, we come to His power. Perfection of warrior strength is His. Glory and majesty—attributes of deity—are His. He is called the "most Mighty" (v. 3), and hero worship in His case is allowable. He is far beyond any of the so-called superstars.

As the girding of the sword was associated with a royal inauguration, we have here a picture of Christ vindicating His claims. In verses 3–5 we have a powerful sword, a triumphant procession, and a victorious rule. Christ's invincible sword is the Word of God.

The language used of the Hero-Monarch in His triumphal war takes us to the Book of Revelation, where we find Christ going forth to conquer all His foes in order to establish His kingdom of righteousness on the earth. And no cruel lust of conquest or mere vulgar ambition will inspire Him as it did the dictators who started World War II. The three virtues harnessed to His chariot are "truth and meekness and righteousness" (v. 4). He will prosper because of these noble qualities. Temporarily, truth is ridiculed, meekness is oppressed, and righteousness is slain; but our majestic Christ will see to their vindication. By His right hand—signifying positional powers—He will carry out all His decrees.

Three short, abrupt phrases depict the confusion and swiftness His battle charge produces: "Thy right hand shall teach thee terrible things," "Thine arrows are sharp in the heart of the King's enemies," and "The people fall under thee" (vv. 4, 5).

Sword and arrows! Our King is the Master of all weapons. None of them are blunt and pointless; all are sharp and able thereby to pierce vital parts. His arrows are sure never to miss the mark. And when He returns as the conquering Monarch, seated on His white horse for His crowning battle, both men and nations will know His power (see Rev. 19:11-16).

The question is, Are we available in the spiritual war for Him to use in His battle to overcome the forces of darkness? It was thus He used Peter on the Day of Pentecost, and over three thousand people fell unto Him.

### *Deity of the King (vv. 6, 7)*

Five key words—*empire, eternity, equity, establishment,* and *exultation*—summarize verses 6 and 7. These words tell of Christ's eternal reign and its consequent gladness. Who can fail to see Christ in all His essential glory and deity, and in the eternity of His kingdom?

Can we take it in? God addresses God! God the Father is saying to God the Son, "Thy throne, O God, is for ever and ever" (v. 6). Yes, and His is a "right scepter" (v. 6). He is the lawful Monarch.

Christ is no usurper. His kingdom will yet be recognized when founded upon righteousness. When He does appear as the King of Kings, it will not be as an earthly dictator, hungry for power and guilty of tyrannical oppression. Righteousness will be the animating principle of His rule.

And He has the double qualification of a perfect sovereign—He can love and hate. What opposites, yet they meet in Christ! He can love as strongly as He can hate. Man in his sinful condition hates righteousness and loves wickedness. But Christ and all who truly follow Him love righteousness and hate wickedness.

Pope Gregory VII, under the protection of the Normans, died in the castle of Salerno in May 1085. His last words, based on verse 7, breathe the tragic fulness of his bitter disappointment. "I have loved righteousness and hated iniquity; and therefore I die in exile."

In an oriental feast, oil was poured upon the head of a distinguished guest as a mark of respect. And God will yet honor His Son for all His anguish!

## Dress of the King (v. 8)

The King's wardrobe also is mentioned. His many garments have a peculiar fragrance of myrrh, aloes, and cassia. Everything about Christ is delightful to our every sense. Even the odor of His apparel is not of blood and battle, unless we think of the blood-dyed garments of judgment of which Isaiah foretold (Is. 63:1, 2). It is profitable to examine our Lord's wardrobe, commencing with the swaddling clothes and ending with the wrappings left in the tomb.

By "ivory palaces" we are to understand imperial splendor. Before long our glorious, scent-robed King will turn aside from the realms above and will rule the earth without a rival. And resultant gladness will be His when every knee bows to own His sovereign rule. Gladness, it would seem, is one of the key themes of this happy psalm. Christ has a double gladness, mentioned in both verses 7 and 8. "Gladness and rejoicing" likewise come to all those who, by grace, enter the King's palace (v. 15).

## Daughters of the King (vv. 9–15)

At verse 9, we reach the middle of the psalm. We now come to the queen in all her glory. There is no contradiction between the King's daughter and the queen. It is said of Matilda the Empress that she was the daughter of a king, the mother of a king, and the wife of a king. In verse 9 the church is the queen; in verse 13 she is the daughter of a king; and in verse 16 she is the mother of a king.

Old Testament writers loved to describe the relation between God and Israel using the figure of marriage. In the New Testament, Christ and His church are presented as Bridegroom and bride.

Several glimpses are given of the King's daughters.

1. *They are honorable daughters* (v. 9). To be counted as a child of the King is the greatest honor one can have. And the royal courts know no lack of such noble courtiers. They are at the right hand of the King, meaning they occupy the positions of love, honor, and power. Ophir produced the purest gold of that time, but our regalia is more precious than the purest gold. Our King would not robe us in anything inferior. No wonder the queen adores, loves, and desires such a King.

Let us pause to take in the full picture. The King girds Himself as a warrior, robes Himself with His perfumed and permanent garments, mounts His chariot, hurls His arrows, conquers His foes, ascends his throne, fills His palace with splendor, gathers His courtiers around Him, and bids His bride sit on His right. Surely, all this is prophetic of the union between Christ and His church.

2. *They are obedient daughters* (v. 10). These thrice-privileged ones bend the ear to catch every syllable of the King's command. All their faculties are trained to

hear and obey when He says, "Hearken" (v. 10).

Such obedience must result in an all-surrendering love. Forsaking all others, we must cleave to Jesus only. All ties of a sinful nature must be renounced. We must forget our father's house. Christ demands a complete surrender. Our spiritual heritage becomes more important than our human pedigree. And with ourselves, everything must be subordinate to His all-mastering love.

3. *They are worshiping daughters* (v. 11). The royal rights of the King demand the recognition of His Lordship. The daughters are told to revere and "worship thou him" (v. 11).

As the Lord He desires us to have a beauty like His own. "Fairest Lord Jesus" would have all His children bear His likeness. He greatly desires such a resemblance. "Each one resembled the children of a king" (Judg. 8:18). Is the beauty of Jesus seen in your life and mine?

4. *They are sacrificial daughters* (v. 12). This verse, of course, speaks of the homage of surrounding peoples. Tyre was a Gentile city, and the merchandise of the world will yet be holiness unto the Lord. Wealthy, outside nations will yet entreat Christ's favor. God chose Israel in order that she might bless the world, as she will yet do. The church can only influence the world as she is wholly yielded to her Lord. She cannot conquer the world if she fails to cast the world out of her heart.

5. *They are attractive daughters* (v. 13). As with the King, so with the daughters—all have perfumed garments. As He is, so are we in this world "all glorious within" (v. 13). The best material and the most perfect workmanship are represented in the clothing of "wrought gold" (v. 13). As the King's daughter, she must have dress becoming to her station, and she has it. The glory and

beauty of the bride is the masterpiece of the King's holy art. The church triumphant will be dressed in white. "To her was granted that she should be arrayed in fine linen, clean and white: for the fine linen is the righteousness of saints" (Rev. 19:8).

6. *They are privileged daughters* (v. 14). "Brought unto the King!" What a day that will be when the marriage of the Lamb is celebrated and the King and His queen become one! The psalmist also refers to following virgins who see the King. Pure hearts we must have—*the virgins.* Pure company we must seek—*her companions.* A pure walk we must maintain—*that follow her.*

7. *They are happy daughters* (v. 15). Joy accompanies the wedding feast. "Let us be glad and rejoice, and give honor to him: for the marriage of the Lamb is come" (Rev. 19:7). What a picture this verse gives us of the homecoming of the bride in the air! And in our hearts we have the witness that the King will soon leave His ivory palaces to claim His queen and take her into His palace. Have you the certainty, reader, that you will have the joyful privilege of going into the marriage supper?

## Decree of the King (vv. 16, 17)

The last two verses of this love-psalm affirm the King's twofold decree that His cause will not fail and that He Himself will be held in everlasting remembrance. "Instead of thy fathers shall be thy children" (v. 16). God buries His workmen but carries on His work. He will never leave Himself without a witness. Sometimes we despair when prominent workers are taken, but God knows where to find other princes.

It is fitting that such a kingly psalm should end with

the decree of the King's eternal fame. He is to receive praise in perpetuity. His beauty, glory, majesty, and power will never be forgotten. "Blessing, and honor, and glory, and power, be unto him that sitteth upon the throne, and unto the Lamb for ever and ever" (Rev. 5:13). And to John's kingly doxology we can add that of Paul: "Now unto the King eternal, immortal, invisible, the only wise God, be honor and glory for ever and ever. Amen" (1 Tim. 1:17).

> *Hark! those bursts of acclamation;*
> *Hark! those loud triumphant chords;*
> *Jesus takes the highest station:*
> *Oh, what joy the sight affords!*
> *Crown Him, crown Him!*
> *King of Kings, and Lord of Lords.*

# 9

## The Psalm of the Trinity

### Psalm 46
### The Song of Holy Confidence

Theodore of Mopsuestia said:

> Of other Scriptures most men know nothing. But the Psalms are repeated in private houses, in streets and market places, by those who have learned them by heart, and feel the soothing power of their divine melodies.

When Paula and Eustochium wrote their famous letter to Marcella of Rome, exhorting her to flee from the tumults and distractions of Rome to Bethlehem, they described how the quiet of country life was unbroken save by the chanting of the Psalms. Ploughmen, reapers, and vinedressers alike sang the songs of David as they labored.

### The Psalm and the Saints

The Psalms also greatly influenced Christian homes in the early ages of the church. As Christianity spread and became a power, the Psalms occupied a larger and still larger place.

Prominent among the Psalms, from which saints, martyrs, and leaders gathered much courage and inspiration during most trying periods of church history, is Psalm 46, "The Psalm of Holy Confidence." Demetrius, the Grand Duke of Russia (1350–1389), met the Mongul invaders on the banks of the Don. Although his troops were outnumbered, he renewed his courage by reading aloud this great psalm. He then plunged into battle and totally defeated the Tartars at Kulikovo.

It was this same psalm that inspired Martin Luther's magnificent courage. In moments of trial when the Reformer was cast down in soul, he would say to Melancthon, "Come, Philip, let us sing the Forty-sixth Psalm." It was likewise this psalm that resulted in Luther's battle hymn, "A Mighty Fortress Is Our God."

Oliver Cromwell, the Lord Protector, exhorted his parliament to set their hearts to sing Luther's psalm.

> That is a rare Psalm for Christians and if he set his heart open, and can approve it to God, we *shall* hear him say, "God is our refuge and strength, a very present help in trouble." . . . If Pope or Spaniard, and Devil and all, set themselves against us, yet in the name of the Lord we should destroy them! The Lord of Hosts is with us: the God of Jacob is our refuge.

John Wesley met the approach of death with the language of this stirring psalm on his lips. Bystanders heard Wesley's twice-repeated cry, "The best of all is, God is with us." Throughout his last night he was heard attempting to repeat the words, "The Lord of Hosts is with us; the God of Jacob is our refuge." Early the next morning the mighty revivalist entered heaven.

James Renwick, the last of the gallant seventeenth-century Covenanters to suffer on the scaffold, was only a lad of nineteen when he witnessed the execution of Donald Cargill in the Grassmarket, Edinburgh. Nerved to witness by such a gory sight, Renwick became the soul of the movement among the Cameronians, who disowned the king and declared war against him as the subverter of the religion and liberty of the nation.

During the dreadful "Killing Times," Renwick was captured. On February 7, 1688, he was executed on the same spot where he saw Cargill perish. When taken prisoner, the notes of his last sermon were found in his pocket. They were based on Psalm 46:10. "Be still, and know that I am God: I will be exalted among the heathen, I will be exalted in the earth."

## Two Features of Psalm 46

Approaching a study of this renowned psalm that so many saints and martyrs cast their anchor in, there are two preliminary aspects of it that we must draw attention to.

The first is that it not only begins with God but ends with Him. A characteristic feature of many of the psalms is the way they give God the first place. God is first! And this is as it should be. He must have the first place not only in our lyrics but in our lives. Further, the designation "God" is in the plural form—*Elohim*—which suggests the Trinity. As we are to discover, all three persons of the Godhead can be traced in this psalm.

The other prominent feature of this psalm of confidence in the Mighty One is the threefold occurrence in its eleven verses of the term *Selah* (vv. 3, 7, 11). This term is found only in the Old Testament, where it is used more than seventy times, principally in the Psalms. It indicates a pause in the music both to give the singers breath and to allow time for meditation.

*The Amplified Bible* translates *Selah*, "pause, and think calmly of that." C. H. Spurgeon, in his *Treasury of David*, wrote of the word as meaning, "Rest in contemplation after praise." Then he gives us the lines:

SELAH bids the music rest,
Pause in silence soft and blest;
SELAH bids uplift the strain,
Harps and voices tune again;
SELAH ends the vocal praise,
Still your hearts to God upraise.

Pause in praise to ponder. Is this not a profitable exercise that all of us ought to practice? Often in our public singing, we give utterance to solemn vows we have no intention of fulfilling. In fact, most of us are liars in our congregational praise.

What are these hymns of praise and worship? In the majority of cases they are prayers to God set to music. What a solemn effect it would produce if a preacher, in the middle of the singing of the prayer, "Take my life, and let it be consecrated, Lord, to Thee," asked his congregation to pause and meditate for a moment upon the sacred contract they were asking God to ratify!

### The Song of the Trinity

The eleven verses forming this psalm, sung by the sons of Korah in the service of song in the house of the Lord, fall into three distinct sections, each of which ends with a "Selah." I have named it "The Psalm of the Trinity," and here is my outline for your study:
1. The Power of God the Father (vv. 1–3)
2. The Presence of God the Spirit (vv. 4–7)
3. The Peace of God the Son (vv. 8–11)

## The Power of God the Father (vv. 1–3)

Observe that the opening verse commencing with God portrays Him in a threefold way—"our refuge and strength, a very present help in trouble." Here is one of those biblical three-ply cords that cannot be broken.

*God is our Refuge.* Our shelter from all enemies is not something but *Someone.* The Almighty Father is our invincible, impenetrable Stronghold. All through the Old Testament, the picture of God as our impregnable yet accessible place of retreat is prominent. As the Eternal God, He is our Refuge, our Fortress, our High Tower, our Rock, our Covert, our Hiding Place—figures of speech that have inspired many of our great hymns, one example being "Rock of Ages, Cleft for Me." All other refuges are false, for God the Father alone is all-sufficient as our Defense and equal to all emergencies as we hide in Him.

> *A fortress firm and steadfast rock,*
> *Is God in time of danger;*
> *A shield and sword in every shock,*
> *From foe well-known or stranger.*

Under the Hebrew system, there were six "cities of refuge." To these an Israelite who had killed another unwittingly could flee and be safe from the avenger of blood all the time the high priest lived (Num. 35:9–28). Even so Christ, the smitten Rock, shelters the believing sinner from judgment and from all foes and fear.

Have you the assurance that your fortress is in God? Can you affirm with David, "Thou art my refuge and my portion in the land of the living"? (Ps. 142:5).

*God is our Strength.* As our Refuge, our Father is able to protect us. As our Strength He energizes us, as in Him together with the Son and Holy Spirit we resist Satan and all his hosts. What is the use of being in a strong fortress unless we have sufficient arms to defend us and food to sustain us?

During World War II, when the Americans found themselves outnumbered by the Japanese in the Philippines, General MacArthur was forced to retreat to Australia to plan further campaigns against the foe. As he left General Wainwright behind, MacArthur uttered those memorable, prophetic words, "I shall return."

Brave General Wainwright gathered what men were left and sheltered them in the Fortress of Corregidor. But there were few arms to defend themselves with and little food to sustain the gallant company. Wainwright surrendered—even although he occupied a fortress. Then commenced that terrible death march, when many courageous American soldiers perished by the way. They had a refuge but little strength. But God our Father is round about us as our Refuge and Protector, and He is in us as our Strength and Provider.

*God is our very present Help in trouble.* Refuge, Strength, Help—what more do we need? The original Hebrew is most emphatic here. It indicates "an exceeding or superlative help in difficulties." That God is ever close at our side guaranteeing our safety is emphasized by the words *very present*. *Very* means actual, real, veritable; *present* suggests in view, at hand and not elsewhere. God is ever at hand to protect and provide.

He is nearer than the nearest, nearer than our trials, and close at our side to bless. Yes, He is present most when He seems absent, controlling all things for our good and His glory. As the Lord of Hosts, He is with us and *in* us. "God is in the midst of her . . . God shall help her" (v. 5). Well might we be found praying at all times:

> *When other helpers fail and comforts flee,*
> *Help of the helpless, O abide with me.*

Knowing our God of protection, provision, and presence (as the first verse describes Him) begets the utmost confidence and courage, "Therefore will not we fear" (v. 2). The reader will notice the psalmist's constant use of *therefore*. Whenever we meet this adverb, we must stop and ask, "Now, what is it *there for*?" The word *therefore* means "for that reason," "because of that," "for that end."

With God in our hearts and on our side, how irrational any semblance of fear is. Faith and fear cannot exist together. When we believe in and accept the full revelation of His love, care, power and abundance, then no matter what crises may arise, the heart will not be afraid. The Lord is our Strength.

The psalmist then goes on to show that even amid convulsion and catastrophic change of all things visible, we shall not be moved because of a faith fixed on our unmovable God. "Though the earth be removed" (v. 2), was the phrase John Wesley preached on when an earthquake shook London, March 8, 1750. This is why Psalm 46 became known as "The Earthquake Psalm." In commemoration of this event Charles Wesley composed a hymn based on his brother's sermon, a verse of which reads:

> *How happy then are we,*
> *Who build, O Lord, on Thee!*
> *What can our foundation shock?*
> *Though shatter'd earth remove.*
> *Stands our city on a rock,*
> *On the rock of heavenly love.*

Along with "the earth be removed," we have the phrases "though the mountains be carried into the midst of the sea, though the waters thereof roar and be troubled, though the mountains shake with the swelling thereof" (vv. 2, 3). Doesn't this sound like a vivid description of the destruction that would overtake the earth in a nuclear war? But these most terrible fears within the range of imagination can describe the upheavals and revolutions among humanity: terrorism, guerilla warfare, the upsurge of nationalism, the overthrow and destruction of nations and dynasties, the demoralizing of society, the persecution and massacre of saints, industrial turmoil, lawlessness, and the rapid spread of all aspects of crime.

Whatever changes and dangers may come, all who are within the divine refuge can meet the tumult of the destructive storms with a confidence born of faith in God's omnipotence. In the days of evil tidings they are not moved. Why? Their hearts are fixed, trusting in the Lord. No wonder David exclaims at the end of this turbulent section, *Selah*! Think of that! Pause and think calmly that no matter what might come, and must come, we have no ground for fear since our Father, the Creator of the rolling spheres, is our Guard and Defense. We can face the worst without dread when the God of Jacob is our Refuge.

> *A sure stronghold our God is He,*
> *A timely shield and weapon;*
> *Our help He'll be, and set us free*
> *From every ill can happen.*

## The Presence of God the Spirit (vv. 4–7)

In the first verse we found a *Refuge*; in the fourth

verse, we find a *River*. We are in need of both. While there may be an allusion to an actual river such as Kidron or the waters of Shiloah, the language of the psalmist must be understood in a figurative sense as well. The Bible leaves us in no doubt as to the symbolism of the river bringing gladness to the occupants of the city.

Did not Jesus refer to the Holy Spirit as a well of water springing up within the believer, and as rivers of water flowing out of his innermost being? (see John 4:14; 7:38). God is spoken of as a "fountain of living waters" (Jer. 2:13), and Christ is pictured as a fountain opened for sin and uncleanness (see Zech. 13:1). The Holy Spirit proceeds eternally from God the Father. He is sent by the Father and Son and shares fully their deity. He is, therefore, "a pure river of water of life, clear as crystal, proceeding out of the throne of God and of the Lamb" (Rev. 22:1).

As for the streams of this river, one old preacher identified them as the *perfections* of God, the *fulness* of Christ, the *operations* of the Spirit, and these running in the *channel* of the *covenant of promise*. Although in David's mind Jerusalem was the "city of God" benefiting from the fertilizing and never-failing river, John used the same language to describe the true church of God. "I... saw the holy city, new Jerusalem, coming down from God out of heaven, prepared as a bride adorned for her husband" (Rev. 21:2). The particular ministry of the river is to *make glad* the divine city, the holy place of the tabernacles of the Most High.

The fruit of the Spirit is joy, and we joy in God through the Holy Spirit. Many a citizen of the heavenly Jerusalem would sink under the stress and strain of modern life were it not for the constant refreshment, joy, and strength that the quickening Spirit makes possible. Amid so much that would sadden our hearts, He gladdens.

*God is in the midst of her.* Has not God the Spirit sojourned in the midst of the church as the source and center of her life and activity ever since He brought her to birth at Pentecost? Ever since her inception, the church has been besieged by adversaries and adversities, but the mighty Holy Spirit has ever been at hand to help and to make her more than a conqueror. What a defiant, triumphant phrase this is: *"She shall not be moved."* How can the church of the living God be dislodged or demolished when within her dwells the invincible Holy Spirit!

One of the obsessions of communism is the abolition of Christianity the church represents. But the communists won't succeed! Nero tried to destroy the church in her infancy by cruelly murdering her devoted members, but the blood of martyrs became the seed of a still more powerful church. And nobody since has been able to destroy her. Yes, I am aware that within the church herself there are some theologians and even pastors whose conception of the role of the church and the kind of message she ought to present to a lost world are entirely alien to the New Testament. But foes without and within the organized church can in no way affect the position of that living organism. The church is His Body, and *she shall not be moved!* Within her is the One who brought her into being. *Tried* she may be, but *destroyed* she cannot be—for she is the dwelling place of God in the Spirit.

Further, what a precious thought is latent in the words, *"and that right early"* (v. 5), or as the margin reading has it, "when the morning appeareth." There are times when it seems as if the Lord Jesus Christ tarries in the deliverance of His persecuted church, and impatience complains of divine delays. But He is never slack concerning His promise. When as the Sun of Righteousness He arises with healing in His wings, then He will remove His church altogether from a godless, hostile world. She will hear His musical voice when He appears, saying, "Arise, my love, my fair one, and come away" (Song 2:13), and she will be caught up to meet her Bridegroom in the air.

Meantime, let the heathen rage and the kingdoms be moved. There never has been such international turmoil and confusion as at this hour. With the upsurge of nationalism and the ever-increasing spread of communism, kingdoms are being moved; but a word from the King of nations, the Comforter, will rule the storm.

Then, at the sound of the trumpet the earth will melt as we await Christ's return to reign forever as the Prince of the kings of the earth. Meanwhile, we can rest and rejoice in the fact that as "the LORD of hosts," the divine Presence is with us as our protector and as "the God of Jacob." He is our impregnable defense. *Selah*! Yes, pause and think calmly of the blessed fact that the Holy Spirit is with us till that day and that He is greater than all our foes and fears.

### The Peace of God the Son (vv. 8–11)

The Lord Jesus Christ alone fits into this definite, prophetic section of the psalm, which is classed among the imprecatory, or judgment, psalms.

There are those who insist that such psalms do not breathe a "Christian spirit" because of their punishments and woes pronounced upon the wicked. They forget, it seems, that our merciful God is also a Judge.

These psalms, however, are not exclusively related to a Christian age but to a just judgment period when the wrath of God will be manifested toward the blatant rejectors of His grace and mercy. What must be borne in mind is the fact that many of the judgment portions of the Bible carry both a present and a future application.

For instance, in David's time the Lord made desolate the foes of Israel. Proud empires like Assyria and Babylon were made to crumble through divine interposition. Wars against God's ancient people were made to cease. But verses 8 and 9 have yet to be fulfilled to the letter. Thus, alongside verse 8 we can make the notation: "Seven Years—The Great Tribulation." In the margin of verse 9, we can write: "A Thousand Years—Christ's Millennial Reign."

In verses 2 and 3 we had the convulsions and desolations in the created sphere. Once the powers of nature are unleashed, havoc and destruction of life and property are experienced. But in verse 8 we have the manifestations of God's judgment-works, which will be so intense during the Great Tribulation era as to cause the recipients of divine wrath to hide themselves from the great Judge of all the earth (see Rev. 6:12–17).

Then in verse 9 we have the emergence of a mighty Conqueror with power to banish war from the ends of the earth. This is exactly what Christ will do when He returns to earth at the end of the Tribulation era to usher in His glorious reign of peace. Coming as the Prince of Peace, the scepter of universal sovereignty will rest in His pierced hand, and war dare not raise its bloody head again (see Is. 2:4). The Peacemaker will have the prerogative of piling war weapons, heaps on heaps, and destroying them all. For one thousand years, this blood-soaked earth of ours will be free of war.

Presently, Christ is not exalted among the nations of the earth. From countless multitudes glory is not ascending to God. There is a lamentable absence of peace on earth and goodwill toward men. But when Jesus reigns from shore to shore—and not until then— the angelic doxology will find fulfilment. Exaltation as the King of Kings and Lord of Lords, will be the Savior's, as He takes unto Himself His right and power to rule the millennial nations. How glorious His ultimate victory will be when every tongue shall confess Him as Lord of all!

Meantime, as we linger amid the shadows awaiting His appearing, how must we act? The Lord Himself tells us, "Be still, and know that I am God" (v. 10). We cannot have a heart destitute of all fear unless we rest in Him who is our Refuge, Strength, and Help. *The Amplified Bible* translates the above phrase thus: "Let be and be still, and know—recognize and understand—that I am God."

Often we are still, but it is the stillness of fear or sorrow or unbelief. In contrast, the thought of relaxation is arresting. The French version of "be still" reads *Cessez*, or "stop it"! Stop doubting, worrying, fussing, and fuming—as if we had a God no greater than international and national upheavals and lacking in power to cope with our personal problems and needs.

> Be still, my soul! thy God doth undertake
> To guide the future as He has the past:
> Thy hope, thy confidence let nothing shake:
> All now mysterious shall be bright at last.
> Be still, my soul; the waves and winds still know
> His voice who ruled them while He dwelt below.

The psalmist goes on to describe the revelations of the Almighty One, in whom we are to rest. He is "the

LORD of hosts" and "the God of Jacob" (v. 11). What vast resources of power and authority are resident in this dual designation repeated by David in this ancient psalm (see vv. 7, 11).

*The LORD of hosts is with us!* One of the names of Christ is *Emmanuel*, meaning "God with us." How significant is the plural here—"Hosts"! He is not only supreme in one sphere but in every realm. "He doeth according to his will in the army of heaven, and among the inhabitants of the earth: and none can stay his hand, or say unto him, What doest thou?" (Dan. 4:35).

C. H. Spurgeon comments:

> The Lord rules the angels, the stars, the elements, and all the hosts of Heaven; and the Heaven of heavens are under His sway. The armies of men though they know it not are made to subserve His will. This Generalissimo of the forces of the land, and the Lord High Admiral of the seas, is on our side—our august Ally; woe unto those who fight against Him, for they shall flee like smoke before the wind when He gives the word to scatter them!

Since He is Lord of *all* hosts, this means He is Lord of all angelic hosts, all stellar hosts, all human hosts, and any other kinds of hosts in the universe. In addition, He is Lord of all satanic hosts. Let not this aspect of divine sovereignty be forgotten. Satan, the leader of hellish hosts, is subservient to the will of God (see John 12:31; 16:11). He is like a dog on a leash, able to go so far but not farther.

Is this not the teaching of the Book of Job? When God gave Satan permission to test His servant, He set the limit beyond which Satan could not go. At Calvary, Satan became a defeated foe, and by faith he can be resisted and bruised under our feet. In the days of His flesh, Christ was triumphant over the tempter and manifested His power over the demons the Devil commanded.

Yes, Jesus Christ is the Lord of all hosts, and we must learn to rest in Him and share His supremacy. Is it not dishonoring to doubt His power and to allow worry and fear to rob us of all we have in Him? With such a great God as our heavenly Father, why should we charge our souls with care? Why do we fuss and fume, mope and mistrust when things go wrong and trials come? Why do we act as if the God we profess to believe in is no bigger than our trials or adversities? Confessed Job, "I know that thou canst do every thing" (Job 42:2). Because this is so, let us strive to rest in the power of God.

*The God of Jacob is our Refuge.* This further aspect of the divine character is most comforting to faith. Why not the God of *Abraham* or *Isaac*? Why Jacob? Why not even the patriarch's new name, *Israel*? *Jacob* means "the heel" because of what happened at his birth, with Esau his twin brother. The name implies "he that supplants" or undermines, cheats or deceives. And Jacob was a trickster. Later, his name was changed to *Israel*, which signifies "a prince with God," or "prevailing with God" (see Gen. 32:28; 35:10).

Why, then, employ the designation twice in this psalm, *the God of Jacob*? Perhaps David felt, as we do, that there is still a good deal of the "Jacob-nature" within our beings, and it is heartening to know that with all our frailties and failures God is our God and "will be our guide even unto death," and through death to glory (Ps. 48:14). "Happy is he that hath the God of Jacob for his help" (Ps. 146:5). Knowing our frames and remembering that we are but dust, God still loves us and cares for us. He constantly strives to wean us from all that is Jacob-like and fashion us into His true Israel.

Three times in the psalm God is pictured as our Refuge (vv. 1, 7, 11)—a fact worthy of repetition. This is an aspect of the divine character. "God is known in her palaces for a refuge" (Ps. 48:3). Selah! Pause and think calmly of Him who is our Lord Protector.

Let us hug to our hearts the revelation of the Godhead as found in this "Song of Holy Confidence." Amid the increasing darkness of the present age, may we be found resting in the power of God the Father, realizing the presence of God the Spirit, and receiving the peace of God the Son. Awaiting His return as the Prince of Peace, may ours be the inner peace nothing can disturb nor destroy.

> *Peace, perfect peace,*
> *In this dark world of sin?*
> *The blood of Jesus whispers,*
> *Peace within.*

# 10

## The Psalm of Our Great King

*Psalm 48*
*A Song of Deliverance*

The reader might be puzzled about the background of this psalm. The author and exact date of Psalm 48 are unknown, and we cannot dogmatically link it to any one event in Jewish history. Reference to "the ships of Tarshish" (v. 7) has prompted some writers to connect the psalm with the overthrow of Ammon, Moab, and Edom in the reign of Jehoshaphat (see 2 Chron. 20:35,36). Other scholars suggest that Psalms 46, 47, and 48 celebrate the deliverance of Jerusalem from Sennacherib (see Is. 37). Both Psalm 47 and 48 speak of God as the "great King" (47:2; 48:2). John Ruskin observed that Psalm 48, along with Psalms 72 and 75, contains "the law and the prophecy of all just government."

The psalm, as a whole, magnifies God as the One who is supreme in every realm. It is like a cabinet displaying the manifold attributes of God. The Spirit-inspired mind of the psalmist soars to the heights as he meditates upon the divine character and being. Thus, the pregnant phrase "This God is our God" (v. 14) provides a fitting climax to such an exultant song. *This God*!

Who is this particular God who is perpetually ours? We find out in this song that seems to be about Jerusalem. Actually, the focus is on the Protector of the Holy City. The psalm in its entirety provides a description of the nature and attributes of God. We can imagine the writer's deep feelings when, after extolling God for all He is in Himself and all He is able to accomplish, he realized that such a God was his very own God for time and eternity.

### *This God!—His Greatness*

How magnificent is the opening phrase of this psalm: "Great is the LORD." Because He is intrinsically great, everything leaving His hand bears the imprint of His greatness.

In *Twelfth Night*, Shakespeare enjoins us not to be afraid of greatness. "Some men are born great, some achieve greatness, and some have greatness thrust upon them." The self-evident witness of Scripture and history is that God's Son was born great, achieved greatness by His life, death, and resurrection, and all through the ages has had greatness thrust upon Him because of the conquests of His gospel. Edward Young, 1721, in *The Revenge* wrote the line, "Great let me call him, for he conquered." Cannot every redeemed soul say, "Great is the Lord, for He hath conquered me"?

A Latin proverb, *Maximus in minimis*, meaning, "Very great in very small matters," can be aptly ascribed to Him who has done *great things* for us for which we are glad. Nothing in life is beyond His ken. His concern and care cover the transcendent and trifling aspects of your pilgrimage and mine.

"Be great in act as you have been in thought," says Shakespeare in *King Richard II*, and the Lord is great in His major and minor acts, since He is ever great in thought. The misled Ephesians cried, "Great is Diana," but our great God is greater than the greatest, and His name shall be great unto the ends of the earth. His greatness is indeed "unsearchable" (Ps. 145:3). "Great is our Lord, and of great power: his understanding is infinite" (Ps. 147:5).

## This God!—His Universal Praise

Because He is great, He is to be greatly or highly praised, not only in His own city but "unto the ends of the earth" (v. 10). Among the world's inhabitants, only His own chosen people in "the mountain of His holiness" can adore and praise Him as He should be. While His enemies, whom He scatters by their own fears, may be forced to recognize His greatness, His own redeemed children can sing as no others are able to, "How great Thou art!" The vast majority throughout the earth fail to meditate upon His greatness in creation, redemption, and providence.

But while man and woman, His masterpieces in creation, fail to laud and honor Him, His other works praise Him for His supreme greatness. Sun, moon, stars, and birds are forever singing His praise.

## This God!—His Holiness

Not all the great of earth have been holy, just as all the holy have not been great in the esteem of the public. But the Lord is both great and holy; He is great because He is holy. Is not *holiness* His most conspicuous attribute? As

123

the psalmist penned this notable psalm by "the city of our God," he had in mind Jerusalem, the peculiar abode of the God of Israel. The beautiful city typified Jewish patriotism and pride. As for the "mountain of His holiness," such was the temple within the city wherein holy priests ministered unto Him, and holy sacrifices were offered unto Him, and holy praises ascended to Him for His greatness in essence, power, wisdom, justice, love, and mercy.

What Jerusalem was, so is the church of the living God spiritually. Bought with the price of the blood of His Son, she is near to His heart. As a temple, she is adorned with His holiness, all within her partaking of such holiness. If Jerusalem was the world's star, is not the true church the most precious pearl of all? Despised she may be by those who see no beauty in her, but she remains as the salt of the earth.

### *This God!—His Sovereignty*

Three times in the Psalms our great God is presented as the "great King" (47:2; 48:2; 95:3). He is greater than the greatest sovereigns who ever reigned. He is "higher than the kings of the earth" (89:27).

United, confederate kings may appear to be powerful, but how limited is their role alongside the sovereignty of Him who is the Potentate of time. Kings, nobles, and others come and go, but our great King continues as the Lord of years. Before long, the nations of the earth will be under the control of Him who is coming as *the* King of Kings. With Jerusalem as the seat of His government, He will reign in peace and righteousness.

## This God!—His Protection

As the Lord, He has *preeminence*; as the King, He has *power*; as the Refuge, He affords *protection*. Solomon once commented on the rabbit-like cony: "The conies are but a feeble folk, yet make they their houses in the rocks" (Prov. 30:26). Weak in themselves, they are secure in the rocks. God has been known all down the ages as a Refuge for His people from all their trials and fears. He is likewise a covert from divine wrath for sinners who seek His grace. Other refuge have we none. He only is our Rock.

## This God!—His Supremacy

What a vivid description the psalmist gives us of God's supremacy over men and nature (vv. 4–8)! While this section may be related to the gathering of Assyrians around the walls of the sacred city and God's great deliverance of His people, it is illustrative of how ignominious foes flee from our all-glorious Victor, whose authority is ever of old.

The Assyrians came and saw the city, even to the counting of its towers; but they did not conquer it. God arose on behalf of His threatened people. The haste of the Assyrians in coming to destroy them was nothing to their hurry in fleeing as judgment fell. Panic and fright gripped them, and the invaders took to their heels. The common expression of fear, "pain, as of a woman in travail" (v. 6), was used by Orientals to express extremity of anguish. It is fitting here. When God puts forth His power, the proudest of foes are made to tremble.

His supremacy is also seen in His ability to command the forces of nature to obey His will, as when He uses the east wind to destroy "the ships of Tarshish" (v. 7). It is said that the sea has only one king—God. What destruction there is when the powers of nature are unleashed! As easily as vessels are shipwrecked when violent winds arise, so God can wreck human inventions, schemes, and ambitions. His breath can speedily destroy everything that is alien to His mind and will.

How safe we are in the hands of Him who is the Master of ocean, earth, and sky! He is Lord of all the universe.

### This God!—His Faithfulness

Unlike primitive tribes, we don't have to fear a fickle and capricious deity. All God has been, He is and will ever be. He is unchangeable in His character and in the fulfilment of His promises. Blessed is the man who has not only heard but seen for himself how great the Lord is. Almightiness and Sovereignty are His as the Lord of hosts; and since He is our God we have the manifestation of His condescension in bringing us into covenant relationship with Himself.

Further, all He establishes is "for ever" (v. 8). His provision is in full harmony with His own eternity. No wonder the psalmist exclaimed, *"Selah"*! What else can we do but pause to praise as we think of all His past goodness, present grace, and prospective glory! Are you among the number who have both heard and seen (see John 4:42)?

### This God!—His Lovingkindness

The psalmist *thought* on the precious theme of divine

"lovingkindness" (v. 9). Here the word *thought* carries the idea of patient waiting with full trust in the Lord and no repining at His delays.

What are the ingredients of His lovingkindness? Can we not name pity for the sinful, pardon for the repentant, grace and power for the believer, and comfort for the tried and afflicted? No doubt you have received some or all of these blessings. The recipients of such bounty should never tire of declaring His unfailing kindness. As assembled saints constitute a living temple— the temple of God—how fitting it is when we gather together that we muse upon His lovingkindness as personally experienced. Praise is ever due His name for all He so freely showers upon our unworthy heads.

### This God!—His Righteousness

By the phrase "Thy name" (v. 10) we are to understand God's manifested character. As the Righteous One, He does not act contrary to His own nature. His right hand, therefore, is full of righteousness; and such divine righteousness was vindicated in the righteous cause of His people at the overthrow of the godless Assyrians. Zion likewise will rejoice because His judgments are true and just, and such righteous acts will always be legitimate subjects for joyful praise (see Rev. 19:1-3).

There is no contradiction between His lovingkindness and His justice. If love is not just, it is not the love reflected at Calvary where love and justice met. We rejoice in the fact that as the Judge of all the earth, He ever does that which is right. His is the justice of omnipotence, omnipotence controlled by justice.

## This God!—His Guidance

Notice the glowing description of Zion's ramparts in verses 12 and 13. See how its inhabitants are no longer imprisoned within its walls because of the fear of a defiant enemy without. They are able to move about freely and cherish what they had almost lost. As the citizens numbered the towers and found them intact, the people proclaimed the goodness of God in preserving them and their city from destruction. The inhabitants of the Holy City wanted the generations to come to know that their deliverance was a pledge of future protection. God was the Guide of Israel "even unto death," delivering the people when their end seemed imminent.

A symbolic application of the towers and bulwarks is hard to resist. Origen saw in them "those doctrines of the true faith, which are the strength and glory of the Church, which are to be maintained in their soundness and stability against the assault of heretical teachers, so that they may be transmitted unimpaired to following generations."

You might find them to be symbols of Christ Himself, the innumerable promises of God, as well as His presence, providence, and covenants: these are the bulwarks of the church. It is a most profitable exercise to go round the spiritual Zion as Israel marched around Jericho, and constantly meditate upon the origin, history, security, privileges, and glory of that great city, the holy Jerusalem, "prepared as a bride," descending "out of heaven from God" (Rev. 21:2,10). Mark well her divine battlements. Anticipate the security and eternal joy offered with those walls.

Because of all that God had done on behalf of His

ancient people, they had little inclination to forget Him or desire to change Him for another. Such a covenant-keeping God would be theirs for ever and ever. With such a display of the virtues and attributes of God as this psalm presents, it is no wonder that the psalmist exclaims: "This God is our God for ever and ever" (v. 14).

Not all can subscribe to this profession of faith. The God of the Bible is not their own personal God. Here we have the language of a relationship that borders on ownership, as when a marriage partner talks about *my* husband or *my* wife. See also a later psalm, "God, even our own God, shall bless us" (Ps. 67:6). Such a relationship gives spiritual stability and emotional affirmation.

"This God . . . will be our guide even unto death" (v. 14). The Hebrew language of this verse is more expressive than English. The Hebrew says that when we reach life's latest hour, the Guide will be at hand to "lead us over death to resurrection." As another psalm puts it, "Thou shalt guide me with thy counsel, and afterward receive me to glory" (Ps. 73:24). Throughout our pilgrimage, the Lord guides and guards us continually, and when the end of the road is reached He is still there to lead us to the living fountains of waters above.

# 11

## The Psalm on Revival

### Psalm 85
### An Anthem of Restored Blessing

Oliver Cromwell seemed to have been fond of using the language of the Psalms. On September 16, 1656, the day before the opening of the Second Parliament of the Protectorate, he sat in his Palace of Whitehall, reading and meditating upon Psalm 85. At the opening of Parliament, the Lord Protector addressed the assembled members. In the course of his speech he said:

> Yesterday I did read a psalm which truly may not unbecome both me to tell you of, and you to observe. It is the 85th Psalm; it is very instructive and significant; though I do but a little touch upon it, I desire your perusal and pleasure.

Cromwell then went on to expound to Parliament his vision of hope: to bring about God's will on earth and to make England an emblem of heaven, where God's will reigns supreme.

### A Drama of Reawakening

Professor Richard S. Moulton groups this psalm along with what he calls *dramatic anthems*, which are psalms exhibiting "a peculiar combination of dramatic movement with the lyric form of anthem. They are so far dramatic that they present a dramatic transition from trouble to relief."

Without doubt, this revival psalm was a prayer of a patriot for the afflicted country he loved; perhaps it was used as a national anthem. Although dedicated to the sons of Korah, it is quite likely that the psalm was penned when the land was oppressed by the Philistines and the people of God were overwhelmed by sorrow, despair, and bondage. If David was its author, then in the spirit of prophecy he foretold the peaceful years of his own reign and of the illustrious rule of Solomon, his son and successor.

A few writers claim that the psalm describes the captivity of Israel and her deliverance under Zerubbabel. But the psalm is not only a sigh of persecuted Israel. It is prophetical of the peace and blessedness of the rule of Christ, both now and during the millennial era.

Such is the mysterious composition of this psalm. Having no date nor name, it can be used in any age, particularly in our own. Amid today's universal spiritual declension, there is a heart-hunger on the part of true saints for a manifestation of God's presence and power in revival blessing. Note the key verse of the psalm: "Wilt thou not revive us again: that thy people may rejoice in thee?" (v. 6). This is surely the cry of many laborers in the vineyard as they realize how blinded multitudes are by the god of this world. As we are to see, the psalm is made up of three distinguishable stanzas.

1. Praise for Former Mercies—*Remembrance* (vv. 1–3)

2. Prayer for Restored Favor—*Revival* (vv. 4-7)
3. Prospect of Future Blessing—*Reward* (vv. 8-13)

*Praise for Former Mercies (vv. 1-3)*

A striking feature of this first section is the employment of "thou hast" six times in the first three verses. Past tokens of divine favor are recalled. What great things God had accomplished for and through His people!

*Thou hast been favorable unto thy land.* Canaan is in the mind of the writer as being God's land, one He had dealt graciously with. Israel found it to be a land flowing with milk and honey. How good God has been to the so-called Christian lands of history. Britain has a long record of God's reviving grace, as has America. I pray that both countries may be renewed in Christ once again.

*Thou hast brought back the captivity of Jacob.* Because of her sin, Israel suffered bondage again and again. But when under the heel of the oppressor, she cried unto the Lord. He delivered her. There have been times when the church was fettered with the shackles of a dead professionalism, intolerance, wealth and prestige. God graciously raised up leaders like Luther and Wesley to break such fetters.

"Thou hast forgiven the iniquity of thy people; thou hast covered all their sin" (v. 2). At the end of verse 2, we have the only *Selah* in this psalm, and it is certainly rightly placed. *Selah*—stop and clearly realize what that means! The psalmist is not thinking of God's forgiveness of the ungodly as they turn to Him in penitence and faith but of His own sinning people. The psalmist, recalling his own heritage, writes of a people whom God had called into a holy priesthood but who had failed Him (read Psalm 106).

Yet because of the multitude of His mercies, God forgave His people again and again. What a God of forgivenesses He was and ever is! (See Eph. 4:32; 1 John 1:7,9.) *The Amplified Bible* translates verse 3 this way: "You have withdrawn all Your wrath and indignation. You have turned away from the blazing anger [which You had let loose]."

There is no inconsistency between God's love and His righteous indignation. He is *holy,* uniting in Himself all the unapproachable perfections of deity. As the Holy One of Israel, He had entered into covenant relationship with a nation in order to fashion it into "an holy people." *Righteous* as well as holy, God as the Lawgiver demanded obedience and determined punishment for transgression of His commands. Thus God, ever slow to anger, was just when provoked by the terrible sin of His people against His holiness and righteousness. At Calvary, God's love was manifested, His justice and righteousness were vindicated, and His wrath was appeased.

> *The tempest's awful voice was heard,*
> *O Christ, it broke on Thee.*

All in Christ have been delivered from "the wrath of God" reserved against unrepentant sinners (see John 3:36), who are still "vessels of wrath" or "children of wrath" (Rom. 9:22; Eph. 2:3). May God send a Holy Ghost revival, that multitudes of these may be saved from the wrath to come! Past displays of God's grace and goodness, then, are the best arguments for believing that He will deal mercifully with all who seek Him.

Because He has ever been "mindful" of His people, He will ever be ready to "bless" them (see Ps. 115:12).

### *Prayer for Restored Favor (vv. 4–7)*

The prayers of the Bible never grow old. After centuries of use, they are still fresh as they leave our lips. What prayer could we pray in these days when the witness of the church seems to count for so little in a world of need? Nothing could be more fitting than the petition for the quickening influences of the Spirit of God found in the middle stanza of this psalm! Use these brief expressions from Psalm 85 as your own: "turn us," "revive us," "show us," and "grant us."

In the opening phrase in the psalmist's sigh for revival we see that repentance of heart is a beginning to spiritual quickening. "Turn us, O God of our salvation" (v. 4). We cannot turn on our own initiative because we are too weak and inert. Convicted of our utter insufficiency, powerlessness, carnality, and sin, we must cry to God to move our hearts toward Himself.

Further, divine rage ceases when our rebellion ceases. And because our impoverishment affects not only our own generation but future generations, how imperative it is for Christ's church today to be a fit recipient and channel of revival.

The echo of wedding vows can be heard in verses 5 and 6, which ask "wilt thou" three times. "Wilt thou not revive us again: that thy people may rejoice in thee?" (v. 6). Because the world is guilty of making void God's laws, it is necessary for Him to work. May He revive His church "in the midst of the years" (Hab. 3:2). *Revival* is the appropriate word for the saved who are backslidden. You cannot revive anything that is dead. Revival implies restoring. Life is within, but it is faint and feeble and needs quickening. The unsaved are dead in sin and therefore destitute of the life of God within. They require *regeneration*.

There is a great difference between a hospital and a graveyard. In the latter there are the dead who cannot be revived, but in the former there are living men and women sick and physically impotent seeking restoration of health and usefulness. The church is like a spiritual hospital. It is full of those who are spiritually weak and need the reviving touch of the Divine Physician, who alone can revive His own.

*Revival*, which the church must have if her voice is to be effective in a world of increasing unbelief and iniquity, cannot be worked up. It must be prayed down. Since it is of God who has His set times to favor Zion, it can be prayed down. Evangelistic campaigns can be successfully arranged. Long and careful planning, skillful advertising, underwriting of all financial costs, and the provision of effective gospel preaching and singing can assure the presence of crowds and also converts. But a pentecostal outpouring, such as was experienced during the great revivals of the last two centuries, cannot be programmed. It comes suddenly from heaven in overpowering conviction and mighty blessing.

There must be, of course, a prepared people ready for such a divine visitation. Revival comes from God in answer to the prevailing intercession of His saints and in response to their unwavering faith and abandonment of all known hindrances to the movement of the Spirit. Consciousness of need, distress on account of it, and confidence that God will come in all His quickening power: these prepare the way for the manifestation of a great spiritual upheaval.

A revival, then, means the demonstration of a divine work in the quickening of saints and in the growing of untiring sacrificial service. As the God of salvation, He likewise moves upon the unsaved, individually, convicting them of their sin. As they repent and believe, He reveals His mercy—perfect in nature, comprehensive in extent, eminent in degree. He removes guilt. He forgives.

May God revive His church and prepare her to assist Him when He brings multitudes into the valley of decision!

### Prospect of Future Blessing (vv. 8–13)

Look at the past when you want to understand the future. Past demonstrations of the power and favor of God are prophetic of all He stands ready to accomplish. Thus, in the concluding section of Psalm 85, we have the manifold rewards accruing from a divine visitation upon an adjusted and prepared church. When revived, she is ready to listen to God's voice and obey Him implicitly. As the God of peace, His own should be at peace with Him and at peace among themselves.

The often bitter divisions and estrangements within the church do not provide the kind of atmosphere in which yearnings for revival thrive. The psalmist speaks of those who have been revived by the Lord and are in right standing with Him when he warns, "but let them not turn again to folly" (v. 8). All bridges must be destroyed. Past grievances must not be repeated. God's Spirit is ever ready to be appropriated in an ever-increasing measure by those who experience a full salvation.

Israel was glorious when she was faithful to her Lord,

137

basking in His manifested presence. When disloyal, she became dishonored. The glory of the Lord departed from her. A striking feature of this revival psalm is that God marshals all His transcendent attributes to bless His captive people. *Mercy* makes her covenant with *truth*, and *righteousness* kisses *peace* reverently.

In a very real sense, mercy and truth met together at the cross of Christ. Through Jesus' death, *righteousness* and *peace* kissed each other. In Christ, *truth* sprang out of the earth, for He condescended to be born of a woman, and *righteousness* came down from heaven. The word "spring" is a metaphor taken from nature—fruit and flowers springing from the earth with the ensuing harvest of joy.

It is thus that the last two verses of the psalm abound with the fruits of a revival. Repentance and divine forgiveness banish desolation; they result in prosperity —not only spiritual but material good. *Glory* dwells in the land where God is fully honored. What kind of glory is implied?

By *glory* an Israelite understood the shekinah glory, or the manifested presence of God. When revival comes— and may it be soon—God will be glorified, worshiped, and obeyed. At present, some church leaders are seeking to destroy His image and reduce Him to a mathematical proposition. When revival comes, there will be an outburst of *moral glory*. God's work in the souls of men ever makes for righteousness. Vice, profanity, ungodliness, and social evils vanish as darkness before light. The revival under Wesley resulted not only in the salvation of souls but in the uplift of society as a whole.

When revival comes there will be *national glory*, for righteousness alone can exalt a nation. Britain experienced her greatest glory when she sought to honor God in furthering His cause among the nations.

When revival comes, there will be *material glory*: "Our land shall yield her increase" (v. 12). When the people praise the Lord, "*Then* shall the earth yield her increase" (Ps. 67:6). God never withholds that which is good from those who walk uprightly. When righteousness goes before Him and He has a people adjusted to His holy mind and will, blessings shower down. His footsteps constitute a way in which to walk. He "shall set us in the way of his steps" (v. 13).

> *Revive Thy work, O Lord:*
> *Now to Thy saints appear;*
> *Oh, speak with power to ev'ry soul,*
> *And let Thy people hear.*

# 12

## *The Psalm of Our Divine Ally*

### *Psalm 124*
### *The Exile's Song of Deliverance*

This stirring hymn of thankfulness is called "A Song of Degrees [Ascents]." We have no doubt whatever that it was written by David. By songs of ascent, we mean those hymns or psalms that were sung by the ancient Hebrews as they marched up or ascended the hill of Mt. Zion to worship God in His temple.

There are those scholars who affirm that Psalm 124 was composed by King David after the tragic death of his rebellious son, Absalom. If this is its background, it proves that David was the recipient of providential deliverances. The Lord was on his side, and he escaped out of the snare of fowlers.

What a marvelous Ally God is! We can afford to be indifferent as to which people are on our side, so long as He is. There may be very few who are willing to stand with us in our effort to be separated unto God, but one with Him is ever in the majority.

### *Ifs and Thens*

This psalm starts with *if*. The repetition of *if* is significant. It is human. But from the divine standpoint,

141

there are no *ifs* in the matter: God is on our side if we are on His. One of the last things John Wesley said was, "The best of all is, God is with us." It is because the Lord is our Protector and Companion that we have immunity from cunning, malicious foes. Tossed about we may be, but never submerged.

Following the *ifs* we find a trio of *thens*:

Then they had swallowed us up quick [alive] (v. 3).
Then the waters had overwhelmed us (v. 4).
Then the proud waters had gone over our soul (v. 5).

The illustration David uses of the steadily rising flood and the hurried rushing torrent or stream may have been suggested by the irresistible rising of the river Nile. Behind the symbol of the proud waters and mighty waves threatening to sink a vessel, we may have a reference to the proud, haughty, rebellious son, Absalom.

For ourselves, the turbulent waters can represent floods of opposition, temptation, and sin. Demonic forces beat against our frail boat. The fact that we are God's children does not mean that we shall not be tossed about by fears within and foes without.

Some of the saintliest souls have been the sorest sufferers. What is taught by this ancient psalm is that in spite of all antagonistic forces arrayed against us, the Lord is our strong Ally, ever ready to preserve us. When Edward Irving, a famous Church of Scotland preacher, was deposed from the ministry, he was spared the pain of hearing himself cast out by the Church that disowned his service. Because of this, Irving said, "I sang in my heart, 'Blessed be the Lord, who hath not given us as a prey to their teeth.'"

Suffering in this psalm is set forth with *water* as its word picture. The waters often appear to overwhelm us, to drown us out. Let us consider this fivefold flood, and the victory that comes as we are rescued by God.

1. *The Waters of Temptation.* Satan is the hellish fowler who sets many a snare to catch the believer off guard. Don't underestimate his skill. Having been snaring souls for almost six millennia now, he is a past master at setting subtle traps. Alas, with respect to Bathsheba, David knew what it was to succumb to the whirling waters of sensual passion! He now writes as one escaping as a bird from the fowler whose snare was broken by the Mighty Deliverer.

There is an old seal in existence, which was once the property of a Huguenot refugee, bearing an imprint of a broken net and a bird soaring upward. The motto reads: "My soul is escaped as a bird out of the snares of the fowler." With the Lord on our side we are more than conquerors when assailed by the enemy of the soul. Thanks be unto God, who gives us the victory!

2. *The Waters of Reproach.* If our lives have fallen unto us in pleasant places and we are continually surrounded by those who are sympathetic toward our Christian witness because of their own love for the truth, we should be found praising God. Not many believers enjoy such a trouble-free environment. Many saints live in an utterly godless home. They discover His constant grace is necessary to testify amid ridicule and contempt. Often we are reproached for the sake of Jesus, whose own heart was broken by reproach. The wrath of the godless is "kindled against us" (v. 3). We would go under if it were not for the consciousness of the Lord's supporting grace.

143

> See round Thine ark the hungry billows curling,
> See how Thy foes their banners are unfurling;
> Lord, while their darts envenomed they are hurling,
> Thou canst preserve us.

3. *The Waters of Disappointment.* Such proud waters dashed against David's soul when Absalom—his proud, conceited son—stole the hearts of the people and sought to rob his father of the throne. Surely this base ingratitude on the part of the rebellious boy was enough to overwhelm the father's heart. But he emerged from the billows in triumph. God had seen to it that His child was not given as a prey to the wicked.

Can it be that you have been buffeted about by waves of disappointment? A shattered idol lies at your feet. Relatives and friends have been guilty of strange actions, cutting you to the quick. At times it would seem as if a disappointed love would go over your soul and submerge you altogether. But there He was—the disappointed Christ, who said of those He sought to love and win, "How often would I have gathered thy children together . . . ye would not" (Luke 13:34). Christ is near at hand to comfort and console your broken heart.

4. *The Waters of Suffering.* To some it seems that if personal foes don't rise up against them and seek to destroy them, physical infirmities afflict them. Suffering almost defeats them. Some dear souls go under because of the pressure of unrelieved pain, yielding to doubt regarding God's love and goodness. They succumb to this snare of the fowler. The prolonged suffering of many a saint is one of the mysteries of life that only our presence in heaven will solve.

Meantime, however, He who created heaven and

earth became the Man of Sorrows, who is fully acquainted with our grief and infirmities and who is now near the pain stricken. The sympathizing Jesus ever seeks to prove the sufficiency of His grace.

5. *The Waters of Death.* The swellings of Jordan await us all unless the Lord should come and spare us from dying. But when the torrents swirl through the valley of the shadow of death, all is well if we are His. He is on our side, and we shall fear no evil. Our souls will escape from the sins and limitations of this life, and our Helper will see us safely home.

As you review this psalm of our Divine Ally, note three ideas:

> 1. The testimony of the past—"The LORD who was on our side" (v. 2).
>
> 2. The triumph of the present—"The snare is broken" (v. 7).
>
> 3. The trust for the future—"Our help is in the name of the LORD" (v. 8).

Use this three-stranded rope. With such a threefold cord, we should never yield to defeat or despair. Let the proud waters roar, wicked men gnash their teeth, and the satanic fowler do his utmost to snare us. We, too, will say we have escaped, for the Lord was on our side. If He be for us, who can be against us?

Boldly we say: "The Lord is my helper, I will not fear what man shall do unto me" (Heb. 13:6).

# 13

## The Psalm of Humility and Hope

*Psalm 131*
*A Song of the Quiet Soul*

You might wonder if it is worthwhile to spend time in the study of a psalm of only three verses. Yes, study and you will find the psalm is *multum in parvo*—"much in little." Made up of only three verses, it is as blessed as it is brief—a short and sweet psalm. Actually, it is composed of two triplet stanzas of a personal nature, and a final couplet of a national character.

A further feature of Psalm 131 is the fact that it is one of a group of fifteen psalms (120–135) known as *The Songs of Ascent*. The title of this miniature psalter within the Psalter is somewhat suggestive. It literally means, as we noted in the previous chapter, "Songs of the Going Up." It is said to be associated with the fifteen steps of the temple, with the Levites singing a psalm on each step as they ascended.

These particular psalms may also have been associated with Israel as the people returned from the captivity of Babylon with humbled hearts, weaned from their idols. The Ascent Psalms have also been connected with pilgrimages to Jerusalem for the great feasts there.

David was the author of this psalm. Many incidents were gathered from his life to illustrate the psalm. Because Israel is likewise spoken of as a weaned child (v. 2, see also Is. 28:9), there is the larger application of this poem, full of the most perfect and sincere resignation to the nation of which David was an integral part. If all the other psalms from the pen of the gifted psalmist **are** gems, this short one is a pearl to adorn our necks in these days of human pride and restlessness. Its sixty words are as a ladder enabling us to climb from deep humility to a fixed and eternal confidence.

Such a distinctive psalm, containing the cry of a child's heart, is intensely personal and is a privilege for other eyes to read. It hardly seems a discourse to be read in public; rather, it constitutes a private conversation with the Lord. I have named it "The Psalm of Humility and Hope," since the first two verses breathe the air of profoundest humility and submission to God's will, and the last verse encourages the child of God to maintain a lively hope in God and His sustaining grace.

## A Humble Heart

David's confession of humility was not the kind of Uriah Heep who contrived to be "'umble." It is sadly possible to be proud of one's "humility." The opening verse is in the form of a private, personal confession. It comes from one who has penetrated the hidden recesses of his being and found pride gone. The apostle Paul also learned that lowliness is one of the highest attainments in the life of a believer. He wrote: "Mind not high things, but condescend to men of low estate" (Rom. 12:16).

David disclaims three distinct kinds of pride, all of which should be foreign to a sanctified heart.

148

1. *There was freedom from secret conceit of heart:* "My heart is not haughty" (v. 1).

When David, as a youth, came to the scene of conflict with Goliath, his brothers rebuked him for his pride. The eldest said, "I know thy pride, and the naughtiness of thine heart; for thou art come down that thou mightest see the battle" (1 Sam. 17:28). But he was unjustly condemned; the opposite was the case. David rose to great heights, yet he was never unduly elated by prosperity. Whatever faults he may have had, pride was not one of them.

With another king of Israel, it was different. The record has it that Hezekiah's heart "was lifted up" with pride (2 Chron. 32:25). Pride, which has God's particular hatred, is a common vice that assumes many forms. Pride is destructive of the soul's true happiness. When David assumed humility before the Lord, he was not pretending. None knew better than he that haughtiness of heart caused many to fall.

2. *There was freedom from fleshly ambition:* "Nor mine eyes lofty" (v. 1).

In Psalm 101:5 we find David saying, "Him that hath a high look and a proud heart will not I suffer." Haughty hearts and lofty looks are pairs common to several psalms. Solomon, David's son, warns us against "a proud look" (Prov. 6:17). Because the eye is the mirror of the soul, there is often a world of meaning in a single glance. What the heart desires, the eye searches for.

A conceited heart is not long in revealing itself in a proud look and lofty bearing. Pride of manner is ever contemptible, especially in a Christian. Apart from divine grace, we are nothing and have nothing. Happy, then, is the man who bears the likeness of Him who was meek and lowly in heart. Our Master did not have a proud look, but in His eyes was compassion for a lost world.

3. *There was freedom from presumption:* "Neither do I exercise myself in great matters, or in things too high [wonderful] for me" (v. 1).

David was wrongly blamed for leaving his father's sheep for the excitement of the battlefield. But the shepherd lad knew his limitations and never journeyed beyond them.

Those who are the Lord's should be content to walk by faith and not try to pry into matters that God has not revealed. There is a presumptuous intrusion that is not of faith. Unprofitable meddling in the mysteries of life often creates doubt. The psalmist said, in effect, "I will never meddle with high schemes, with matters far beyond me."

Many of us commit the common sin of attempting too much, of undertaking tasks beyond our wisdom and ability. Qualified simply to sweep a floor, we want to rule a kingdom. Does not David in a later psalm speak of knowledge "too wonderful" for him—so high that he could not attain it? (see Ps. 139:6).

There are realms so great and high, both in revelation and providence, that reason cannot penetrate them. His ways are higher than our ways. Childlike loving trust learns of God's mysteries that battle the human genius who is often weary and disappointed in the quest. Matters hidden "from the wise and prudent" are revealed "unto babes" (Matt. 11:25).

## A Subdued Will

The metaphor David uses of his soul as a weaned child is as touching and beautiful as it is powerful and expressive. It is interesting to observe that the word introducing the second verse, *surely*, is commonly used to express strong asseveration after an oath. If in the first verse we breathe the air of humility, here we have the beneficial air of contentment. Since the figure David uses is one of the most striking in the Bible, let us examine its full implication. The *Amplified Bible* reads: "Surely I have calmed and quieted my soul, like a weaned child with his mother; like a weaned child is my soul within me."

David likens his calmed, quieted soul to a *child*. Are we not taught that unless we become as little children we cannot enter the kingdom of heaven? A child represents helplessness and dependence upon others. Childlike we must be, but not *childish*. Too many of us are not simple and lowly enough for God to use. We are too big for Him to do anything with. A child is confident of the love of parents and of their care and provision. How the apostle John loved to speak of saints as "little children"!

Further, David thought of himself not only as a child, but as a child *weaned* of its mother. Repetition of the phrase "weaned child" adds emphasis to the lesson of humility. David had been restless and passionate but had learned how to be calm and compose himself. At the time of weaning a child sobs, but as new food becomes palatable the infant ceases to cry and grieve.

Thus, suffering over the mystery of an unexpected refusal and a new method of providential care is at the back of the metaphor used. Several profitable applications can be made of David's illustration of maternal treatment.

First, there is the thought of separation from things the soul once loved—the loss of what was depended on most. Although when a child is weaned he loses what his mother gave, he **does not lose** his mother. So, when the Lord turns us away from some cherished possession, we must not become cross and fretful but ask the Holy Spirit to make us "meek and quiet" (1 Pet. 3:4).

One Christian writer comments:

> Instead of fretting after what is too great for him, he quits his ambition, and his spirit lies calm and gentle, like a child in its mother's arms, after the first trouble of weaning is over, soothed and lulled by the maternal caress.

The child is weaned *on* the mother rather than from her, and still nestles close to her breast. We likewise must be content whenever God takes away a treasure and gives us something else. Often, it is more of Himself.

Secondly, the child is not only separated from the past source of sustenance but ceases to desire it. The child is happy and at rest, although he is no longer allowed what once delighted him. Is ours the delight of surrendering what once delighted us? Sanctification (a word seldom heard these days) is a weaning from sin, self, and worldliness. Sanctification is a willingness to abandon pleasures and pursuits that are not essentially wrong in themselves, but which come between us and the Lord.

How blessed we are when questionable things go and the heart is weaned from the things of earth to things above, from sin to holiness, from self to the Savior! David knew what it was to be weaned from pride and vanity of heart, from a self-confidence deeming oneself generally right and others generally wrong. The psalmist was weaned from all self-will, self-seeking, and self-sufficiency. Objects of satisfaction he formerly sought had lost their hold upon him.

The psalmist, in the third place, also knew that no child is able to wean himself. As God's child, he was dependent upon His Spirit to cause any semblance of pride to become embittered to his taste.

Have not many of us proved that without help we were unable to surrender the world voluntarily but that our sanctification was a work God alone could accomplish? Only God can "sanctify you wholly" (1 Thess. 5:23). Thus, the teaching of the weaned child is evident. It is the rest of faith and love experienced in true submission. The gift is denied, but the mother is still embraced. Can we say that the mood of willing submission is no strain whatever but free and joyous? David said, in effect, "I have soothed and stilled my soul as a mother calms her weaned child."

Often a sucking child is impatient and restless, but the weaned child grows quiet and content to forego the first source of sustenance for a more substantial means of nourishment and growth. The figure David used, then, is plain.

A dedicated scholar said this about the mother's milk:

> It is taken from the baby's first real sorrow when he not merely feels pain, but is allowed no access to that which had been his solace hitherto. He moans, and frets, and sobs, but at last is quieted by the love which is powerful to soothe, even when it must deny. So as George Herbert says of man, "If goodness lead him not, then weariness may toss him to God's breast."

### A Radiant Confidence

Weaned from himself, David thought of others. Delivered from self-thought and self-pride, he lost

153

himself in his care and desire for Israel. "Let Israel hope in the LORD from henceforth and for ever" (v. 3). Separated unto God, David delighted in Him. Assured of His love and salvation, he encouraged others to hope in the eternal God.

The true church has the blessed hope of the return of the Lord for her complete deliverance from a sinning world. Such a glorious hope will soon be fully realized. The past warrants such a confidence; the future will justify such a confidence.

David assured Israel that her hope in the Lord covered the present and the future. As the covenant God, the God of Israel, He was the encouragement to hope. Because of all He is in Himself, He cannot fail those who trust in Him. There is always room for the largest hope when we are weaned from every aspect of pride. Humility feeds hope. David knew and taught (when an outlaw because of Saul's jealousy) that although he was the anointed king over Israel, he could patiently and quietly wait for the crown designed for him. In this psalm, he counsels Israel to emulate his example.

If we are fully weaned from all that prevents our spiritual growth, we shall find it good to hope and quietly wait for the salvation of the Lord. The tranquil Christ alone can impart this calm.

> *"Upheld by hope," all toil is sweet*
> *With this glad thought in view,*
> *The Master may appear tonight*
> *To call His servants true.*

# 14

## The Psalm on Christian Unity

*Psalm 133*

*A Song As Valued As a Precious Pearl*

In praise of unity and brotherly harmony, this exquisite sonnet is referred to by Professor Moulton as "A Song of Unity in view of the gatherings from all over the land at the sacred feast." In these days when Roman Catholic and Protestant leaders are concentrating upon the unity of the church, it is important to go back to this ancient psalm—another "Song of Ascents"—in order to discover the true basis of union.

Matthew Henry says that some writers conjecture that this psalm was composed by David upon the occasion of the union between the tribes when they all met unanimously to make him king.

The tribes of Israel had long had separate interests during the government of the Judges; but now they were united under one common head, now the Ark was fixed, and with it the place of their rendezvous for public worship and the centre of their unity. Now let them live in love.

It is evident that the author of this sparkling sonnet

155

knew from bitter experience the folly and futility of disunion in home, church, and state. The author gave us this most precious pearl of a psalm, which should be read along with John 17.

The background of the psalm accounts for the joy felt in the reuniting of Israel after long disunion arising from the disruption of captivity. Various classes of pilgrims (the spiritual and secular authorities, the rich and poor, citizens and peasants) went on a pilgrimage three times a year. Such intercommunion of pilgrims fostered a unity of feeling and sentiment. Scattered century after century, it was good and pleasant to be reunited after the separation and depression of bondage. Palestine, both north and south, had been torn by strife, discord, and war. Now David writes as if all the tribes are bound together as one family in the unity of the national and religious life.

How happy the heart, home, church, and nation into which such unity comes and abides! The special feature of Psalm 133 is the way it magnifies the excellence of the grace of unity among the saints of God.

## The Substance of Unity

The trinity of verses composing the psalm commences with the particular society or community called upon to manifest unity—*brethren* (v. 1). What exactly is meant by this designation? Sons of a family are brothers and contribute to a happy home when they strive to live in unity.

We hear much these days about the brotherhood of man. Statesmen claim that all people are brothers and sisters; therefore, we should seek to live in peace regardless of the color of our skin.

But as used by David, *brethren* has a religious connotation equivalent to what Jesus meant when He said, "One is your Master, even Christ; and all ye are brethren" (Matt. 23:8). This special understanding is what Peter had in mind when he advocated "unfeigned love of the brethren" (1 Pet. 1:22, see 5:9). Unless Christ is our Savior and Master, leading us to the Father, we are *not* included in the spiritual brotherhood He Himself had in mind. Such a relationship comes as a result of regeneration when we are made children of God and, therefore, spiritual brothers.

Thus, my understanding of the word differs from that of the politician. I believe *brethren* is a term including the saints of God in any or every place. Unity among *them* is what Jesus prayed for in His High Priestly Prayer, "that they may be one" (John 17:22). Why don't we heed His prayer? Such a fellowship of believing hearts is so precious and sacred a bond that lack of harmony is a disgrace. "He that soweth discord among brethren" is an abomination unto the Lord (Prov. 6:19). May it be our constant endeavor "to keep the unity of the Spirit in the bond of peace" (Eph. 4:3).

Before the inspired writer got to the word *brethren*, he began the sentence with the exclamation, "*Behold!*" (v. 1). Does this not suggest that unity is somewhat rare and, therefore, admirable where found? Satan's constant tactic is to divide and conquer. He is more than active today destroying harmony in the home, the church, and the world.

Further, the exclamation indicates some manifestation of loving union David had witnessed. True unity, when seen, is admired; it influences those who behold it (see

Gen. 13:5–18). May "brotherly love" and union become more common among the children of God (see Heb. 13:1)!

Such unity, says David, is *good* and *pleasant* (v. 1). The combination of these two adjectives indicates the substance and influence of unity wherever it reigns. Some things are good and beneficial but not pleasant, such as bitter-tasting medicine. Other things are pleasant but not good. The tree looked pleasant to the eyes of Eve, but eating of its forbidden fruit was disastrous for the human race (see Gen. 3:6). But with the unity David extols, both qualities are in harmony.

*It is good.* Spiritually and morally, unity is always good in the work and influence of the church, and in the lives of its members. United, we are able to stand against the dark forces of evil. A church hopelessly divided finds it extremely difficult to reconcile a torn and broken world to God.

*It is pleasant.* Discord and strife are ruinous and always bad and unpleasant. On the other hand, unity among the people of God is always attractive. Nowhere has the true nature and influence of unity, where Christians are bound together not by artificial restraints but by Spirit-begotten unity of heart, been more gracefully stated than here in this brief psalm. The spectacle of saints fighting each other is neither good nor pleasant for God's work in the world. How dishonoring to the Lord is a church divided by useless discussion and fierce feuds.

To "dwell together" means to live continually together in unity. Is this not something totally different from a mere artificial, superficial, organized union that we concoct? We are to dwell together even as one, having one heart, one soul, one passion. We are to live in peace and harmony as one in Christ Jesus. Such oneness of heart, aim, and aspiration gives unity its strength and reward.

In the time of Augustine, it was this psalm about the beneficial end of unity that helped to give birth to the monasteries. The monastic system gave a trumpet call to those who wished to withdraw from the world and live together as brethren or friars. Although in the course of the years monastic life changed, its original intention was good and noble.

Perhaps, at this point, it is fitting to distinguish between *unity* and *uniformity*. Dwelling together in unity does not mean that we are rubber-stamped into a similar form. One of the failures of communism is its effort to destroy individuality and to make all people think and act alike.

The unity of the Spirit is no mere outward uniformity. Holy unity is not brought about by mechanical restrictions and regulations that are often monotonous and wearisome. It is not enough to subscribe to a creed and present an external, formal semblance of unity.

The form the Bible speaks of is inherent, substantial, and spiritual. This is the only unity worth fostering because it promotes the glory and kingdom of Christ, and represents a heart-union of cheerful people ready to work together for one supreme purpose, all serving God with their own particular and peculiar personalities and gifts. In an orchestra there may be hundreds of singers and players. Yet in spite of a great diversity of instruments and voices, they can play together in harmony. Thus is it with the church of our Master.

Differing in talents, as one musician differs from another, yet united to the Great Conductor by a common faith and forged into the bond of spiritual unity, each of us may contribute to harmony. Christian unity is certainly needed in a world so destitute of peace and unity.

The world is always impressed with a church in which peace, concord, and the blessed fruits of union are evident. Since we belong to the Lord, we do not have to concoct unity but simply manifest it. Organically, we are already one in Christ Jesus. But the outworking of such an eternal union is not as apparent as it should be. What we are in *position* is not evident in *practice*.

Churches may have the appearance of success—good congregations, sufficient money, ornate buildings, efficient organizations—but of what avail are all these externals if they are destitute of divine blessing? What good are material accumulations if life and service are not offered with a peaceful spirit?

At a time like this, when different religions and denominations are striving to resolve their differences, it must not be forgotten that there can be no unity apart from mutual acceptance of the divinely inspired and infallible Scriptures, adherence to all the fundamental doctrine of the Christian faith, and sanctity of life. How can we walk together if we are not in agreement on these essential matters?

### The Symbols of Unity

Notice two figures in verses 2 and 3. They might seem incomprehensible to an urban church member in the space age. The psalmist uses the figures he knows about from liturgical worship and nature. David likens pleasant brotherly unity to the precious anointing oil used in priestly services. Then he calls attention to the dry land's regular gift of the refreshing dew. One symbol comes from the religious realm; the other, from the natural world.

*The precious ointment.* The psalmist goes to the ritual of Israel for his first illustration of the fragrance of unity. He describes the anointing of Aaron as high priest with the sweet-smelling and all-pervading ointment.

Unity! It is like the precious ointment poured on the head, that ran down on the beard, even the beard of Aaron—the first high priest—that came down upon the collar and skirts of his garments—consecrating his whole body (Ps. 133:2 *Amplified Bible*).

Poured upon the head, the ointment flowed down, diffusing its fragrant odor wherever it traveled until the whole person was sanctified by it. In Scripture, the anointing ointment is typical of the unction of the Spirit, who is the source of unity (see Eph. 4:3,4). The ointment was poured upon Jesus at His baptism and came copiously upon the disciples at Pentecost as they were gathered together with *one* accord. Spiritual union can only come from the Spirit. Divisions, schisms, estrangements among the members of the body of Christ (the anointed Head) indicate the failure to recognize the presence and power of the Holy Spirit.

*The refreshing dew.* The "dew" is used by David as an image of assembling multitudes. The *Amplified Bible* reads:

Like the dew of [lofty] Mount Hermon, and the dew that comes on the hills of Zion; for there the Lord has commanded the blessing, even life for evermore [upon the high and the lowly].

To the Jew of old, the dew or night-mist of Hermon

was considered lovelier and holier than the common dew elsewhere. Thus God's promise to be "as the dew unto Israel" (Hos. 14:5) had special significance. The famed, copious dew of Hermon penetrated garments as well as gardens. In a land of drought, the dew meant marvelous fertility. Legend has it that the Jews would go out at sunrise and gather handfuls of dew as it floated down from the summit of Hermon, covering themselves with it as a remedy for all diseases.

As dew is an expressive emblem of the Spirit's ministry, Spirit-inspired love is the dew that makes for fruitfulness in a barren world. How we need a baptism of the refreshing dews of love—the mighty downpouring of the Spirit's power as ointment. The Spirit, in His descent as dew, refreshes us. The point of comparison is not between the preciousness of the ointment and the fructifying qualities of the dew. Both are said to have come "down"—a key word the psalmist uses three times in two verses, and one that expresses the illimitable influence of unity from above.

Ointment ran down from the head and covered the body of Aaron. Dew descended from Hermon's summit upon the mountain of Zion and the plains below. Both were freely given from above. There was no limit to the utility of both ointment and dew once they were set in downward motion. As the head of Aaron received the ointment that gradually covered his whole being, and as the head of the giant Mount Hermon constantly gathered and dispersed the dew for the fertility of the fields below, so Christ our Head promised us the Holy Spirit without measure, that He might distribute His gifts and graces to all the members of His body, the church.

We have to confess, however, that the visible church

sadly lacks that special unity. The Spirit, as the Holy Oil, waits to permeate her whole life with the pleasant perfume of His sanctifying grace. The Spirit wants to endue the church as with sweet morning dew, with all His refreshing and life-giving power. When and where such Spirit-begotten unity is experienced and manifested, *there* the Lord commands "the blessing, even life for evermore" (v. 3). How He longs to see His dear children happy and harmonious, loving one another and seeking each other's highest welfare!

Does He not testify again and again to His pleasure over peace, concord, and love among those in communion with one another and with Himself? He ever waits to command His blessing upon those who walk in the light of His Word (see Lev. 25:18–21; Deut. 28:8). As the God of peace, He supplies our every need as we live in peace (see Phil. 4:7,9,19).

Rent asunder by schisms and distressed by heresies, the church can yet be purged and revived. When we ask the Holy Spirit to restore the *koinonia* unity of the New Testament to our churches, then we can become a mighty, spiritual force as the shadows of judgment gather around a guilty world.

Blessing one holy Name, partaking of one holy Food, and animated by one blessed hope, the church prepares herself. The unified church, bought by His own blood, will receive His blessings.

May Charles Wesley's prayer for abiding and practical unity be realized by each of us!

*Join us, in one spirit join,*
*Let us still receive of Thine;*
*Still more on Thee we call,*
*Thou who fillest all in all.*

163

*Sweetly may we all agree*
*Touched with loving sympathy;*
*Kindly for each other care;*
*Every member feel his share.*

*Love, like death, hath all destroyed,*
*Rendered all distinctions void;*
*Names, and sects and parties fall,*
*Thou, O Christ, art all in all.*

# 15

## The Psalm of
## the All-searching Eye

*Psalm 139*
*A Majestic Song of the Ever-present Companion*

It was the divine, invisible omnipresence of this remarkable psalm that prompted Carolus Linnaeus, the Swedish botanist (1707–1778), to inscribe over the door of his lecture room: "Live innocently: God is here." One cannot read this most majestic psalm without the overwhelming sense that God is here, there, and everywhere; and that, consequently, we must live innocently.

Aben Ezra, a great Jewish scholar, spoke in A.D. 1056 of Psalm 139 as "The Crown of All the Psalms." Thomas Erskine, Covenanter of Linlathen, wrote of it, "This is the Psalm I should wish to have before me on my deathbed."

I never tire of preaching on this psalm. I find in it some of the most lofty thoughts of God couched in the most sublime language ever used to describe the Almighty. I like to point to Psalm 139 as one of the finest pieces of sacred literature we have today because of its masterly conception of the attributes of God.

C. H. Spurgeon says of this pearl among the expressive hymns of Israel:

> The brightness of this Psalm is like unto a sapphire stone, or Ezekiel's "terrible crystal"; it flames out with such flashes of light as to turn night into day. Like a Pharos, this holy song casts a clear light even unto the uttermost parts of the sea, and warns us against that practical atheism which ignores the presence of God, and so makes shipwreck of the soul.

The psalm was composed, as the heading suggests, by King David, the sweet psalmist of Israel. Its twenty-four verses are made up of four strophes (stanzas) of six verses each, with each section presenting an essential aspect of God's being, as well as an element in the soul's experience of God. Let us, then, note this perfect structure of the psalm.

## The Omniscient One (vv. 1–6)

"Omni" means *all*, and "science" means *knowledge*. God, as the Omniscient One, is perfect in knowledge. Nothing is hid from Him whom some have called "The Eye of the World." No one or no thing is beyond His ken. Life—outward and inward; past, present, and future—is open to Him as a scroll. Our downsitting, uprising, the path we take, our works and words: all are before Him. The soul thus searched and known of God requires no argument that He exists.

Professor Moulton speaks of those psalms with an *"Envelope Structure,* in which the opening and closing lines unite in a single thought of which the intermediate parts are an expansion." Psalm 139 is a fine example of this "envelope structure," the opening protest of which reads, "O Lᴏʀᴅ, thou hast searched me." The concluding prayer reads, "Search me, O God."

On the face of it, it seems as if there is a contradiction here. David commences his psalm by stating that he has been thoroughly searched by God, then concludes by asking God to do something already accomplished. But the above two phrases, as we know, are complementary.

In the first part of the psalm, David is taken up with the exterior of his life such as "downsitting" and "uprising" (v. 2). In respect to the external realm, he confesses that God knows all about this outward sphere. The psalmist, however, journeys on from the exterior to the interior, and feels that there is a world of undiscovered sin within. He prays that God will turn the searchlight on his soul to discover whether there is any wickedness in those darkened cells where passions sometimes reign supreme.

## The Omnipresent One (vv. 7–12)

This further attribute implies that God is everywhere at one and the same time. As the stanza shows, God is everywhere at home, abroad, in heaven and in sheol; in darkness and light; He is at hand night and day. He is the atmosphere of all life. It is in Him that "we live, and move, and have our being" (Acts 17:28). Answering the question, "Whither shall I flee from Him?" Augustine said, "The only way to flee *from* God is to flee *to* God."

From David's praise of God for His omniscience and omnipresence, we infer the overthrow of the powers of darkness. He who sees and hears the abominable works and words of the ungodly will surely deal with them according to His justice.

In his comment on this psalm, Moulton observed that

the movement and dramatic change in the middle are most impressive. The reader should compare verses 1 and 23 in order to evaluate this observation:

At the opening the sense of Divine omniscience and omnipresence is realised as an oppressive burden; in space there is no escaping it, in time it stretches back to birth itself. This climax is also the turning point: as the poem passes into the antistrophe the thought of birth has suggested the omnipresence of God watching the helplessness of the unformed body. The new current of ideas gathers strength, until God's countless thoughts on behalf of the Psalmist have become to him a joy; in a burst of purity he takes sides against the enemies of God; and finally changes the opening burden into an aspiration.

### The Omnipotent One (vv. 13–18)

"Potent" means *power*. Thus, omnipotence is simply God's almightiness. "Touching the Almighty ... he is excellent in power" (Job 37:23). Job said to God, "I know that thou canst do every thing, and that no thought can be withholden from thee" (a verse combining omnipotence and omniscience, Job 42:2).

God not only knows our needs; He is able to meet every one of them. The reason He has such an intimate, personal knowledge is because He fashioned each person by His power. Even in our unborn state we were under the control and guardianship of God, who is the Author of all life—physical, spiritual, and eternal.

### The Just and Holy One (vv. 19–24)

This last section breathes the spirit of holiness, and is related to those forces alien to God's holy will and purpose. He is able to make us holy because of all He is in Himself. Searching out all that is unlike Him, because of His almightiness, *He can transform us into His holy likeness*.

What He reveals, He can remove. But can we truthfully say that we share His just hatred for everything that is foreign to His glorious, unflecked holiness? "Be ye holy; for I am holy" (1 Pet. 1:16). Is it not blessed to know that His commands are His enablings? "Faithful is he that calleth you, who also will *do* it" (1 Thess. 5:24, italics mine).

We must go back, however, to verse 5 of the psalm, which is like a gem in a casket of precious jewels. "You have beset me and shut me in behind and before, and have laid Your hand upon me" (*Amplified Bible*). Such a verse summarizes the truth of the psalm as a whole, for it covers all the attributes we have just considered, and consoles our hearts with the certainty that God is before us, behind us, and beside us.

What a contrast there is between the pronouns at the beginning and the end of the verse—*thou* and *me*. This is as it should be—God first and ourselves last. How full of pronouns this incomparable psalm is! *Thou* occurs eleven times; *thy*, seven; *thee*, six; *thine*, twice.

God is the Omniscient One who sees and knows all our past, present, and future. His "eyes" (v. 16), His "thoughts" (v. 17), His "leading" (v. 24) are all associated with our lives both here and hereafter.

God is the Omnipresent One who is ever with us from birth to burial. When we "awake," we are still with Him (v. 18).

God is the Omnipotent One, and therefore is able to meet the needs of our entire life. He can blot out the past, provide for us in the present, and secure the future.

169

God is the Just and Holy One whose supreme desire is to have a people like unto Himself both in time and eternity. With His holy hand upon us, we can know what it is to walk in holiness before Him.

Further, this all-inclusive verse speaks of divine ambushment, as well as almightiness. The word *beset* means to ambush, surround, encamp, besiege. Ask any veteran of the war in Vietnam. He can tell you what "ambush" means. It is a battle term. When soldiers are besieged or ambushed by the enemy, unless they are skilful enough to extricate themselves from such a perilous position they face surrender or annihilation. But God surrounds us for our protection and preservation. Did He not assure His people of old that He was round about them as the mountains are round about Jerusalem? Ours, then, is the God-encircled life. (See Job 3:23; 14:5,13,16: 19:8.)

It may be that David was thinking of the time when both he and his men were besieged by Saul (1 Sam. 23:8), and of the way God graciously preserved him. Such an ambushment operates both ways—shutting in and shutting out. In the spiritual sense, when we are encircled by God, we are *shut out* or *off* in respect to the world. We are *shut in* with Him who is our Refuge.

When an army or portion of it is thoroughly besieged, all supply lines are severed. In Him we cannot perish with starvation, though cut off from what used to satisfy us. All our supplies are within, even in His all-sufficiency. Thus, forming a circle round His own, He sustains them from within.

Do you object to calling your life "God-besieged"? If not God-besieged, then you are sin-besieged and "easily beset" by sin (Heb. 12:1). Preachers in the past were fond of the saying, "Every Christian is a Christ-enclosed man," as the three Hebrew youths experienced in the fiery furnace. The predominant thought of the psalm, then, is the fact that our lives are surrounded or hedged in by God, and that we cannot flee from Him. May ours be the constant realization and appropriation of all God has provided for us in Himself!

This Almighty God will "lead me in the way everlasting" (v. 24). That way is one of heavenly bliss and free of eternal punishment. All who are saved by grace have been delivered from the wrath to come. As a righteous Judge, He must "slay the wicked" (v. 19). Yet because we are in Christ Jesus, future condemnation will not be ours. He is preparing a place for us in the Father's home and is returning to take us there. Alas, those who are in their sin have no one between them and a lost eternity! If they linger and die in their sin, they will die hopeless, since they rejected their only Mediator.

The believer can say with confidence, "Thou hast laid thine hand upon me" (v. 5). He is a God at hand, protecting as day follows day. Praising Him for all He was to us in the past, we are encouraged to know that He is the same today, and we will know Him even better tomorrow. The eternal God is:

The same *Yesterday*—the God behind me, the God of the ages.
The same *Today*—the God beside me, with His guiding hand.
The same *Forever*—the God before me in the dim, unknown future.

How precious are the lines of Ruth Thomas in her poem, *The Untried Way*:

171

Before me is a future all unknown,
   A path untrod:
Beside me is a Friend well-loved and known,
   That Friend is God:
Before me lies a new and untried way,
   Midst shadows dim:
Beside me is my Guide, and day by day,
   I walk with Him.

Concluding our meditation of this incomparable psalm, I must draw attention to its personal emphasis. David believed that all that God is in Himself was for his own heart. This is why personal pronouns flood the psalm—*me, my, mine* (thirty-two times) and *I* (seventeen times).

Thus, a fitting title of the psalm could be *My Lord and I*. David knew that God had searched *him*; was behind and before *him*; that wherever *he* went God was there; that God's innumerable thoughts were toward *him*; that *he* would be led in the way everlasting.

Is yours this pronoun of personal possession? Can you say, "*This* God is *my* God"? No matter how simple, ordinary, and unknown you may seem to be in the eyes of the world, you can prove the promise, "Thou art ever with me, and all that I have is thine" (Luke 15:31). You can appreciate His divine nearness without feeling guilty or apprehensive. You can give thanks for the affirming companionship of God.

# 16

## The Psalm of Inclusive Praise

*Psalm 150*
*A Song the Atheist Cannot Sing*

The final psalm in the Psalter completes the collection of the hymns of Israel. It ends on an optimistic note of praise. In one way, this word *praise* summarizes the Book of Psalms. It is an all-inclusive word.

The idea of praise is one that is denied to the atheist—that person who has cut himself off from the possibility of admitting the existence of a Superior Being. Thereby, the atheist cannot express any emotion to a Being he claims does not exist. To deny oneself the opportunity of praise—is that not a description of hell itself? Yet the self-worshiping, God-denying atheist has wilfully chosen an eternity without any outflow of praise toward his Creator. Such a dammed-up, decaying life is like the Dead Sea, receiving life-giving waters but passing along no life for mammals to drink or fish to swim in. The life without praise is just such a tragedy.

Note the word *praise*. It occurs two times in every verse of Psalm 150, except in verse 1 where it occurs three times. A total of thirteen times the word echoes through this psalm The verb is used as an imperative command or a loving request.

To the person who has worshiped in the temple, the command is to praise. To one who has found God in the beauties of nature, the command is to praise. To the Hebrew who looks back to the mighty acts of deliverance, the command is to praise. To the Christian who reviews his spiritual testimony—from a gentle wooing by the Holy Spirit, to coming under conviction for sin, to confessing sin and trusting Christ, to following in His blessed teachings and example—the command is to praise. To the person who has listened to the Psalms and meditated on their meaning for contemporary life, the command is to praise.

### Call to Worship (v. 1)

This is another "envelope psalm." It begins and ends with the same idea—a command to "praise ye the LORD" (vv. 1, 6). These words are an emotional request, based on the authority of an experienced believer. They are directed to the heart that has been sensitized by the Savior.

A friend in a southern state writes:

> I attended a youth service one Sunday night. The first words of the worship leader were these: "We are just going to 'hang loose tonight.'" I was stunned by the words—unlike the usual words of the dignified choral or spoken call, such as "The Lord is in His holy temple." But more than just breaking tradition, they made me question how much planning and rehearsal had gone into that service. As the program progessed, the congregation and I found the impromptu, haphazard event showed no preparation, no practice—just hopes that God would bless.

It reminded me of a college roommate who held a student pastorate. He would spend all week long working on his car or playing football. On Sunday morning he would say, "John, pray that the Lord will give me a sermon today."

I don't think we can expect God to bless our laziness. Whether it is a youth service or a college preacher's sermon, I think God wants us to praise Him with our best talents and our best preparation before He sends His Holy Spirit to anoint and bless. I love the dignity and beauty of the Psalmist's loving command, "Praise ye the Lord." It demands my best.

In the call to worship, notice that the expected place of worship is "in his sanctuary" (v. 1). The ancient Hebrew thought first of all of the place set aside where priests and people could meet God. In ancient times it was the tabernacle, built according to God-given specifications. Later it was the temple, the focus of corporate worship for God's chosen people.

Yet God indicated in this inspired psalm that He did not want His praise restricted to the temple. The emotion of praise would be felt beyond the ornate courtyards of the building atop Mount Zion. Where else besides the temple? Look at the all-inclusive answer: "in the firmament of his power" (v. 1). Praise Him in whatever place God has made by His creative power— in other words, everywhere!

## Reasons for Praise (v. 2)

The Christian living in the space age is tempted to forget "his mighty acts" and their influence (v. 2). The news media proclaim various types of energy, from hydroelectric to thermonuclear. Modern man is tempted to forget that behind all these forms of energy stands the great Energizer, because all of these are merely human manipulations of the great power the Creator has placed here. They should not be presumed to be of human invention.

The careful Bible student can never forget the great truth of God's power. In the Old Testament, God commanded that the Passover be celebrated yearly to remind His people of His mighty deeds in rescuing them from bondage. In the New Testament, Paul said, "For as often as ye eat this bread, and drink this cup, ye do show the Lord's death till he come" (1 Cor. 11:26). A grateful Christian will never forget His mighty deeds.

The ideal and aim of this call to prayer is that we should give God His due. "According to his excellent greatness" (v. 2) means recognizing the purity, majesty, power, and lovingkindness of our Holy God.

## Seven Ancient Instruments of Praise (vv. 3–5)

The ancient Hebrews used all sorts of instruments in musical praise of Almighty God. The psalmist listed seven. We can be more sure of the nature of these instruments than were the translators of the *King James Version.* New findings in archaeology and research have identified some of them, but still some of the names are a bit uncertain.

The "trumpet" is actually the ram's horn that sounded alarms, called men into battle, and summoned them to worship. The "psaltery" is a lyre. The "harp" is the stringed instrument that young David learned to play on. The "timbrel" is a hand drum. Inserted in the midst of all these musical instruments is dance—rhythmic movement, coming immediately and logically after the drum that sets the tempo and gives the beat to the music.

The term "stringed instruments" is a general term, and it includes several instruments of this type. The term translated "organs" actually is a general term meaning wind instruments of the flute type. The final words are not exactly certain but seem to mean two kinds of cymbals of different size and volume. Put these all together and what do you get? A mighty sound—not just a noise—of disciplined players giving their best in God's worship service.

### Concluding Call (v. 6)

After the specific instruments have been listed, the psalmist broadens the cry to praise. He extends it to "everything that hath breath" (v. 6). No one need feel left out. To every person who has been given breath—breathed on by the breath of God—there goes the call to acknowledge the Giver of that breath, the Spirit of God. No one is excluded. Every living creature is included.

I am gladdened to see that in modern church buildings such things as railings and ramps are provided for the handicapped. Educational facilities are provided for slow learners and exceptional people. Services include "signing" for the deaf and translation into foreign languages for people who do not speak English. What all this signifies is a marvelous truth: everyone is welcomed in God's house. Each person is encouraged to love and thank the Creator-Redeemer.

This psalm ends with "praise ye the LORD." These words not only end this particular psalm, but serve as a conclusion to Book V of the Psalter. Yet the words of praise summarize and conclude the entire collection of the Psalms, and form a fitting conclusion to our study. We have traveled a long road that included individual psalms of various types and combinations of types. Now, looking back over all of them, we see that one response is called for—praise. The idea is to give God His due. Grant Him from your grateful heart what He deserves.

I hope that after studying these psalms your spiritual life will be enriched and deepened. I hope you will pass along to others the marvelous testimony of your own salvation experience and encourage the skeptics to join you in praising your Redeemer.

I hope you will return again and again to these portions of the Scripture that offer such insight into the human soul and inspiration to the backslidden spirit. Consider this question: If all your life were lived in a spirit of praise, what effect would it have on the world? Try living that psalm-soaked, praise-centered life. You will discover personal growth and satisfaction you never dreamed possible.

"Praise ye the LORD!"